When Lyell Cresswell died on 19 March 2022 – a death hastened by Covid-19 – he had recently completed his third piano concerto and this autobiography.

The concerto completed his catalogue of more than 120 works which includes a dozen other concertos, many instrumental and vocal works, and four operas. In 2016 when he became an Arts Foundation Laureate, he said, 'I find it impossible to tell lies when I'm writing music. I tell my story and give my view of the world.'

Born in 1944, Lyell Cresswell grew up in a Salvation Army family in Wellington, New Zealand. He graduated from Victoria University with a first class honours degree in music before heading overseas for further studies in Toronto, Aberdeen and Utrecht. His career as a freelance composer began to take off when, in 1978, he won the prestigious Ian Whyte Award for his orchestral work *Salm*. Over the years a long list of other prizes, residencies and awards followed.

His music is highly individual and unlike that of his contemporaries. It draws on a wide range of influences, most notably art and literature, but also Celtic and Māori cultures. His works have been played by leading musicians all over the world, although he had particularly close relationships with artists, musicians and orchestras in New Zealand and Scotland, where he lived for most of his adult life with his New Zealand-born wife, Catherine.

His music also inspired his art, including his drawings for *The Magical Wooden Head*. His subversive sense of humour and a deep appreciation of the absurd not only gave rise to exuberant graphic scores and other artworks, but provided entertainment for his family, and a wide circle of friends and colleagues.

Divagations, Doodlings and Downright Lies

Lyell Cresswell

TE HERENGA WAKA
UNIVERSITY PRESS

Te Herenga Waka University Press
Victoria University of Wellington
PO Box 600 Wellington
teherengawakapress.co.nz

First published 2024

Edited for publication by Gillian Whitehead and Scilla Askew

ISBN 978-1-77692-213-0

A catalogue record is available from the National Library of New Zealand

Printed in Singapore by Markono Print Media Pte Ltd

Un livre comme je ne les aime pas,
ceux épars et privés d'architecture.
(This is the kind of book I don't like,
scattered and without architecture.)

Stéphane Mallarmé, Divagations, *Preface*

Doodle to befool, cheat
Doodle to play (the bagpipes)

Shorter Oxford English Dictionary (1987)

Doodle to scrawl or scribble meaninglessly or aimlessly

The Chambers Dictionary (2010)

And, after all, what is a lie? 'Tis but
The truth in masquerade; and I defy
Historians, heroes, lawyers, priests, to put
A fact without some leaven of a lie.

Byron, Don Juan XI. *xxxvii*

It is useless, useless, said the Philosopher,
Life is useless, all useless.
You spend your life working, labouring,
And what do you have to show for it?

Good News Bible, Ecclesiastes 1:2

Piero Casadei

Contents

Acknowledgements

In 2000 Robert Hoskins invited me to give the Massey University Composer Address. I began with four different biographical sketches. These sketches, with some small amendments and the addition of three more, form the basis of the following ramblings. Each sketch is followed by a commentary which goes some way towards disentangling the facts from fantasy. The original address, entitled *Tracing the Lightning Flashes*, was first published by Massey University Music in 2000, and then included in *Finding Language*, a collection of all the Massey composer addresses edited by Michael Brown and published by Victoria University Press (now Te Herenga Waka University Press) in 2017.

I refer to some of my graphic scores, four of which, *Feet*, *Eye Music*, *Body Music*, and *The Magical Wooden Head* drawings, have been published by Wai-te-ata Music Press in the *Anthology of New Zealand Graphic Scores 1984* and *Strange Terrain, a New Anthology of New Zealand Graphic Scores 1965–2023*.

The recollections of my uncle Richard Sharp, edited by my brother Roger Cresswell in 1995, and research into the Cresswell family history by my nephew Jeremy Cresswell, have helped with much of the background family information.

When the Covid-19 pandemic first struck, my wife Catherine and I were in New Zealand. For most of the lockdown we stayed in the idyllic surroundings of Whatamango Bay, Marlborough Sounds, with Don Miller and Helen Ainsworth, Catherine's sister. They were very kind and saved our lives. Much of the background work for this book had been done over some years, but it was during the months of lockdown that it took shape.

Many people have helped me keep on track and others have been happy for me to use material. I should like to thank Tim Thornicroft, Veronica Porter, Maurizio Bottarelli, Ron Butlin, John Cousins, Catherine Cresswell, Jeremy Cresswell, Mary Cresswell,

Max Cresswell, Stephen De Pledge, Fiona Farrell, Elizabeth Kerr, Iain Matheson, Richard N. Russell and Gillian Whitehead.

All photographs and illustrations have been acknowledged throughout. Those that have not are from the family archive or our own collection.

"Ritratto di Lyell" M. Bottarelli 2015

Maurizio Bottarelli

Prelude

Archaeologists encounter maggots, hairy spiders, worms, giant centipedes, snakes, corpses of rats, scuttering vermin and ragbags of skeletal remains as they sift through human rubble with shovels, welded trowels and toothbrushes looking for shards, coins, vessels, tools, figurines, carvings, death masks and any other artefacts. They then label, analyse and interpret them in order to shed light on the lives of people from the past. Creative artists have to trawl through the debris and creepy crawlies of their inner archaeological site to dig out raw material for their work. Composers have to fossick around in this midden to find bits and pieces that can be transmogrified into musical notes. Extreme care must be taken, because every note becomes a living, breathing being.

For some years I have been carrying out an archaeological dig into my own ruins. All the findings so far have been mundane. No gold coins, amulets, rings, necklaces, diadems or jewel-encrusted swords have been unearthed, but there is a lot more work still to be done.

My report on the excavations is contained in the pages that follow.

For Catherine

Chapter 1
Saturday 13 October 1944

> Tell all the Truth but tell it slant –
> Success in Circuit lies
> Too bright for our infirm Delight
> The Truth's superb surprise
>
> *Emily Dickinson*

I was born on Saturday 13 October 1944 in Bethany Hospital, Wellington; the third son of Jack and Muriel Cresswell.

I was brought up on the family farm in the midst of the rich vineyards and tobacco crops of Nelson. The farm, however, was devoted to raising sheep and growing apples. It had been passed down from generation to generation on the understanding that nothing produced on it would be used for the making of wine, beer or cigarettes – the demon drink and the filthy weed.

Bedtime reading for my brothers and me came from the tracts written by our great-grandfather William Cresswell on the biblical justification of temperance. Two tracts in particular were very popular, *A Brief Inquiry into the Truth of the Principles of Abstinence* and *The Testimony of the Word of God against Intoxicating Liquors.*

My father was the local town bandmaster. In the dead of night he could sometimes be glimpsed hunched, under the tungsten lamp, over his writing table. Moving little more than a tuatara, he copied, arranged and composed music for his band – music appropriate for every conceivable occasion. The band comprised a handful of players and a motley assortment of brass instruments, all of which I learned to play. My mother was the local piano teacher. She nourished me with Plunket methods and John Thompson's *Teaching Little Fingers to Play.*

My first experience of music outside this sphere was a concert given in Nelson in 1954 by the Vienna Boys' Choir. The choir had delighted audiences throughout New Zealand with the music of Haydn, Mozart, Schubert, Johann Strauss and a clutch of Austrian folk songs. I was enchanted by the music and agog at the disclosure of a whole new world of music-making by people of my own age. Perhaps this was a defining point in my life and set my resolve to follow a musical career.

But my life was not devoted only to music. The common boyhood country pursuits were another part of it. At the age of 15 I became the New Zealand schoolboy small-bore rifle champion. I was sent to England to shoot for the Lady Gwendolen Guinness prize for boys. I travelled 12,000 miles to fire 12 shots, was beaten for the prize by one point and returned home. This experience kindled within me the desire to travel and confront the wider world. It also flamed my determination always to find the target.

After some years of study at university I worked as a postman, hospital theatre porter and gardener, all the time nurturing an obsession with writing music. I made my way to Europe and set out on the path towards self-sufficiency as a composer.

I was born on Saturday 13 October 1944 in Bethany Hospital, Wellington; the third son of Jack and Muriel Cresswell.

I first saw the light of day in Bethany Hospital on 13 October 1944. The origin of the adage 'Lumen accipe et imperti'[1] is unknown, but it was the motto of the benighted secondary school I attended. My birth took place in the early hours of the morning – around four o'clock. Consequently I was rather slow to accept the light, and once accepted, disinclined to pass it on. The inability to see the light has defined my whole life.

In 1914, 100 years after the birth of my great-great-grandfather Thomas Cresswell in 1814, and 200 years after the birth of my great-great-great-great-great-grandfather James Cresswell in 1714, the Salvation Army opened the Bethany Maternity Hospital at 18 Kensington Street, Te Aro, Wellington. The building, a lovely villa built in 1902, was originally a private dwelling. Around the same

Nº 66391 **NEW ZEALAND** R.G.—103

REGISTRAR-GENERAL'S OFFICE

CERTIFICATE OF DATE OF BIRTH

Certified that, according to the record of the birth in the Registrar-General's office, LYELL RICHARD CRESSWELL *was born at* WELLINGTON *on the* 13TH *day of* OCTOBER, 1944.

GIVEN under the seal of the Registrar-General at Wellington, the 16TH day of NOVEMBER 1964.

REGISTRAR-GENERAL NEW ZEALAND

FEE 2s

CAUTION—Any person who (1) falsifies any of the particulars on this certificate or (2) uses it as true knowing it to be false, is liable to prosecution under the Crimes Act 1908.

40M/8/61/4461/W.P.

time other Bethany Homes were also established throughout the country in Auckland, Russell, Gisborne, Napier, Christchurch and Dunedin.

The main purpose of the hospital was to take care of unmarried mothers, with a view to saving their souls and transforming their lives. They were encouraged to seek moral and spiritual guidance from the staff, who were all members of the Salvation Army and willing to provide this. The mothers were well treated. Once they had given birth they were allowed to stay on without charge. Visits to patients were usually supervised and many of the babies were kept on after the mothers left until they could be adopted out. Abandoned children – those saved from broken relationships and various dreadful situations – were also cared for. The building was extended in 1936 and opened up to fee-paying married mothers in order to provide more funding for the upkeep of the hospital and the care of the unmarried mothers. Married and unmarried women were always kept apart.

My brothers were also born in Bethany hospital – Max in 1939 and Roger in 1942. Max remembers being taken there and peering at me through a glass screen just a day or two after my birth on 13 October 1944. The hospital closed in 1975. Ten years later the building was demolished to clear the way for road alterations to Victoria Street and Webb Street, and the construction of extensions to the motorway.

Some time after my arrival at Bethany Hospital.
With my brothers Max (with glasses) and Roger.
My mother's hair is somewhat like mine in the 1970s.

I was brought up on the family farm in the midst of the rich vineyards and tobacco crops of Nelson. The farm, however was devoted to raising sheep and growing apples. It had been passed down from generation to generation on the understanding that nothing produced on it would be used for the making of wine, beer or cigarettes – the demon drink and the filthy weed.

My great-grandfather acquired a farm in Lower Moutere in 1869. It has remained in the family ever since and is now owned by my cousin Beverly and her husband Ernie Dyke. Though not a legal requirement, the farm was passed down on the understanding that nothing produced on it would be used for the making of wine, beer or cigarettes. I was not brought up there.

As children we sometimes spent our summer holidays on the farm, It comprised an apple orchard, paddocks for sheep, a few hens, some chickens and a cow. There was a tractor shed, an apple packing shed, a lovely big barn, a sheep dip and a farmhouse. Communication with neighbours was by means of a party line telephone. To reach the world beyond, calls had to go through an operator. Each household had its own distinctive ring based on a number and a letter in Morse code, and everyone knew when someone was being called. A crank handle was used to dial the number. There was no privacy, but it was not polite to eavesdrop.

We picked apples, rode on the tractor, chased sheep, tried a hand at milking the cow, played with the dogs, roamed around the farm and watched my uncle remove dags from the sheep. We played on the bouncy bridge over the Moutere River until it collapsed when too many people stood on it for a photograph. Once, feeling the need to stand up like a man and show that I could take it, I watched while my uncle slaughtered a lamb for Christmas dinner.

Now and then, before it was despoiled by tourism interests, we were driven over to Kaiteriteri Beach to play on the dazzling golden sand and flop around in the water. On the way we ran the gauntlet of the wicked hop and tobacco plantations of Riwaka and Motueka. As we sped between these dubious fields at 60 kilometres per hour I felt a tiny, naughty tingle.

Whenever we drove to Motueka we passed the grim wooden meeting house where the Exclusive Brethren gathered. Sometimes we would catch a glimpse of clean-shaven men outside the building in their trilby hats and dark suits without ties in close conversation. The women, draped in long dresses with headscarves covering their long hair, stood submissively behind and the children cowered behind the adults in total silence. There was not a knee in sight. We kept our heads down for fear of being snatched from the car and taken away to be shut up in a room without windows, books, music or radio, and made to fast.

One summer when the family returned to Wellington, I was left in Lower Moutere on my own. With self-imposed secrecy I began writing some music for string quartet. When it seemed that no one was about I would creep into the sitting room, sit at the piano and begin to tinker quietly with some notes. My ears were kept open not only for the music, but also for any sign of voices or creaking floorboards that might lead to my discovery. Ever since I have disliked talking about work in progress. Fortunately this vestigial quartet has been lost.

A family gathering outside the famhouse in Lower Moutere c.1954. From left: Florrie, Muriel, Roger, Great Auntie Oceana, Frank, Ray, Jack, Lyell and Max; front: Vivien, Laurel, Beverly, Frances, David and Alan.

Bedtime reading for my brothers and me came from the tracts written by our great-grandfather William Cresswell on the biblical justification of temperance. Two tracts in particular were very popular, A Brief Inquiry into the Truth of the Principles of Abstinence *and* The Testimony of the Word of God against Intoxicating Liquors.

William Cresswell was born in the village of Lasham in Hampshire, England on Saturday 31 October 1835. He was the son of Thomas and Amelia Cresswell. In January 1842 William and his mother arrived in Nelson not knowing that Thomas, who went before them, had died. At the age of 12 William became an apprentice to a tinsmith. He spent some time in Australia before returning to Nelson, where he married Ann Green Gledhill, became a pillar of the local community and a staunch Methodist. In 1860 he wrote his first temperance tract *The Truth of Love*, and in 1862 he was one of the founding members of the 'Young Men's Mutual Improvement Society'. More tracts followed, including *A Brief Inquiry into the Truth of the Principles of Abstinence* and *The Testimony of the Word of God against Intoxicating Liquors.*

Great-grandmother Ann Cresswell, née Gledhill (d. 1913).

William's tracts were consigned to a trunk in the attic of the old farmhouse, where they lay neglected and unread for many years. They were never brought out for our betterment. More likely bedtime reading might have been *More Adventures of Rupert*, *Panda at the Fair*, *Sama Prince of Elephants*, *The Indian Twins*, *Jennings and Darbishire*, *Biggles in the Baltic*, *Another Job for Biggles*, *Gimlet Bores In*, or passages from the Bible.

My father was the local town bandmaster. In the dead of night he could sometimes be glimpsed hunched, under the tungsten lamp, over his writing table. Moving little more than a tuatara, he copied, arranged and composed music for his band – music appropriate for every conceivable occasion. The band comprised a handful of players and a motley assortment of brass instruments, all of which I learned to play.

My father was not a bandmaster but his brother Ray was bandmaster of the Motueka Salvation Army Band. He sported a special bandmaster's uniform every Sunday with curly white epaulettes. The band comprised six or seven enthusiastic players. It was capable of providing a glorious, rousing and singularly tuned accompaniment to the hymn singing. Ray composed music for the Salvation Army mostly in the form of cheery marches. He was sometimes called 'the Salvation Army Sousa'. During one holiday on the farm I remember seeing him sitting at his desk late in the evening writing by the light of a small lamp above the desk. Perhaps I was on my way to bed with Biggles.

From time to time Ray and his family came up from the farm to visit us in our childhood home in Karori. Once he took me aside and gave me a sheet of empty manuscript paper which I treasured for a long time. His encouragement and his example meant that I understood from the beginning that a composer could be a living being.

Sketch for a hymn tune arrangement for brass band by Ray Cresswell.

My mother was the local piano teacher. She nourished me with Plunket methods and John Thompson's Teaching Little Fingers to Play.

On 14 May 1907, two years and a week after the birth of my mother Muriel Sharp, the Society for the Promotion of the Health of Women and Children was founded in Dunedin. The moving force behind this venture, Frederic Truby King, was born on 1 April 1858. His father Thomas King was the manager of the Bank of New Zealand in New Plymouth. Truby began his working life as a clerk in his father's branch before turning to medicine and going to study in Edinburgh.

The Society for the Promotion of the Health of Women and Children soon became known as the Plunket Society, after Lady Victoria Plunket, wife of the Governor of New Zealand, who gave it her support. Within two years there were branches in Auckland, Wellington, Christchurch and Dunedin. The motto of the society was 'to help the mothers and save the babies'. King, however, held some rather dubious opinions. He was a supporter of the New Zealand Eugenics Education Society, which was established in Dunedin in 1910.

I was indeed nourished with Plunket methods, as was Catherine – many years before we married. She still has her Plunket Society Baby Record. Inside the front cover there is a list entitled 'Your Baby

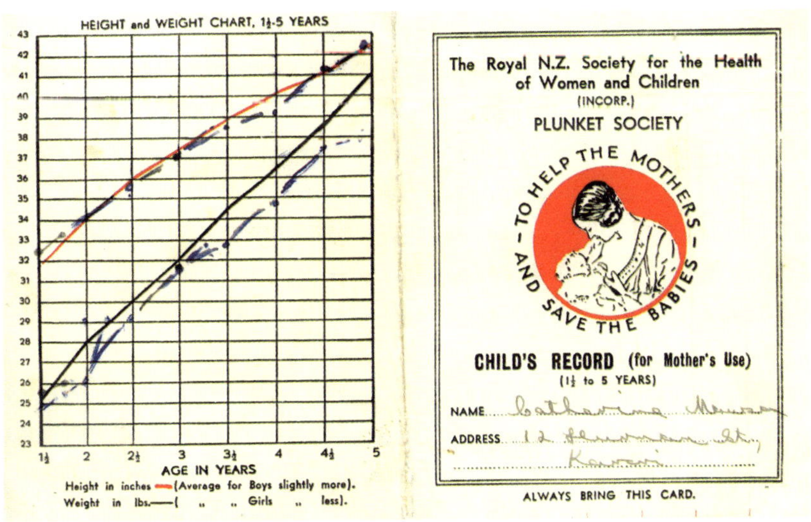

Catherine's Plunket record 1950–52.

Needs'. This list concludes with the note 'Baby must NEVER sleep in bed with his mother'. On the first page of the booklet there is a translation of an old French proverb:

> The most loving act a mother can do is nurse her baby.
> Nothing can ever replace the milk and the heart of the mother.

Some of the entries from the 1949–1950 record:

13.9.49
Increase Kariol to 4 teaspoons
Milk 17 ozs
Water 15 ozs
Karilac 2 tablespoons + 2 teaspoons
Orange juice increase up
4 teaspoons

4.10.49
Small gain
Same recipe
Orange juice 5 teaspoons

8.11.49 4pm
Good progress
Refuses some feeds
Do not force
Try Rose Hip Syrup in her bottle

19.1.50 3.50pm
Length 29 ¼
Head 18 ½
Chest 18
Muscle tone fairly good
Is exiting her solids well
But not so keen on her milk

1.6.50 3.40pm
2nd injection
Cutting 2 teeth
Appetite still poor
Pulls herself up

No date
Brains, fish, liver
3 eggs weekly
Sandwiches for tea
Kariol 3 teasps. Daily

16.8.50 3.10pm
Appetite good
Is waking at night

And from the 1951–52 record:

11.2.52 3.15pm
Seen by Dr put on shoes all the time

14.6.52 3.10pm
Seen by Dr a bonny lass

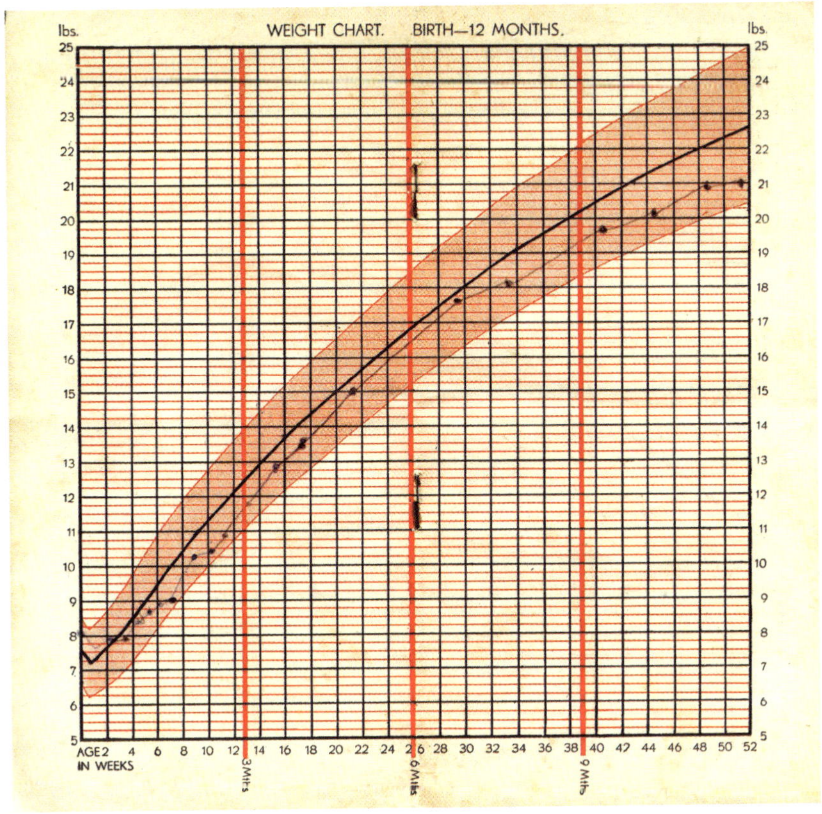

Weight Chart, birth to twelve months.

Kariol, an emulsion, and Karilac, a powder, were added to milk. They were made from formulae devised by Truby King for 'humanising' cows' milk to make it more suitable for babies. As a child I remember being given the vile tasting and slimy textured Lane's Emulsion, which claimed to be 'a reliable remedy for pulmonary diseases, coughs, colds and general disability'. I was unaware of any of these benefits.

The Plunket Society did not advocate playing the music of Mozart to babies. There was no suggestion that music might stimulate emotional, physical or intellectual development, or encourage self-confidence and communication skills.

Childhood was happy, secure and innocent. We played with the usual things – toy soldiers, cap guns, Dinky Toys, Meccano, Hornby trains – and we played marbles, draughts, chess, cops and robbers, cowboys and Indians, and cricket. On Saturday afternoons we were sometimes allowed to go to the 'flicks' at the Regent in Karori, where we saw the *Ma and Pa Kettle* films, *The Three Stooges*, *Robin Hood*, *Batman and Robin*, *Davy Crockett*, *High Noon*, *The Man from Laramie* and the obligatory war films.

Every Sunday we were taken across town to the grandparents' place for lunch, which always consisted of the remains of their Saturday night roast. Then we went off to afternoon Sunday school for homilies, Bible stories, games and songs complete with actions.

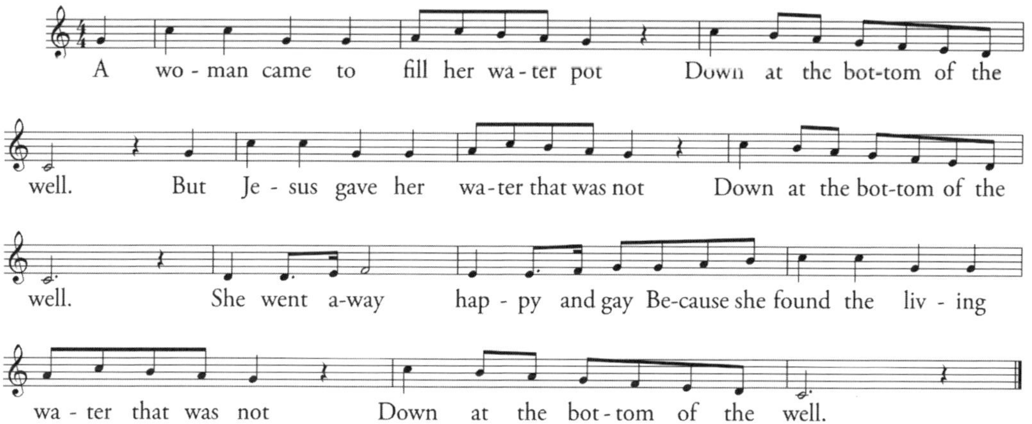

We also sang these songs:

Tangles, tangles, tangles I've been in.
I was born in Tangletown because of Adam's sin.
Jesus came into my heart and undid all the knots.
Now I'm happy 'cos I'm free from tangles.

Ring one, ring two
Ring three and he will hear.
For the saviour's waiting on the hallelujah telephone,
Waiting to answer prayer.

Hear the pennies dropping,
Listen while they fall.
Every one for Jesus,
He shall have them all.
Dropping, dropping,
Dropping, dropping,
Hear the pennies fall.
Every one for Jesus,
He shall have them all.[2]

J-O-Y
J-O-Y
This must surely mean
Jesus first
Yourself last
And others in between.

I'd rather be a little thing climbing up,
Than a big thing coming down.
I'd rather be a junior with a smile,
Than a grown-up with a frown.
I'd rather be poor with a humble crust,
Than rich and lose my crown.
I'd rather be a little thing climbing up,
Than a big thing coming down.

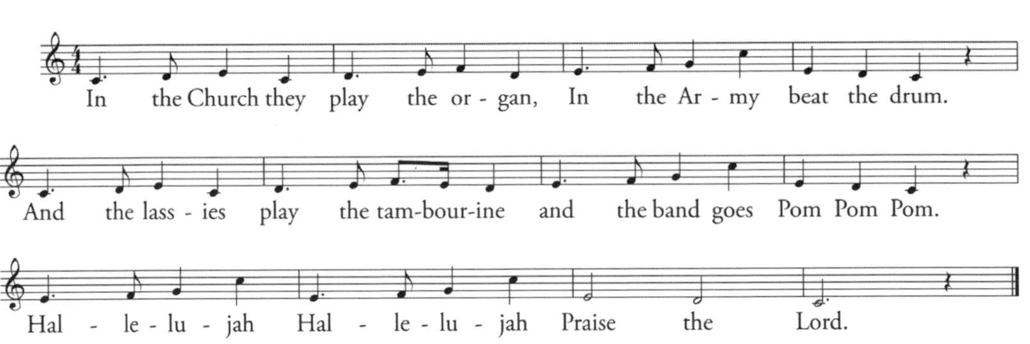

My mother was not a piano teacher, and only very rarely did I hear her play the piano. My earliest memory of any attempt to teach me to play the piano is an unlikely one. Max, my eldest brother, sat at the piano with me and instructed me to play all the F-sharps. It must have made some impression, but I can't say that F-sharp has been a pivotal note in my compositions.

My first experience of music outside this sphere was a concert given in Nelson in 1954 by the Vienna Boys' Choir. The choir had delighted audiences throughout New Zealand with the music of Haydn, Mozart, Schubert, Johann Strauss and a clutch of Austrian folk songs. I was enchanted by the music and agog at the disclosure of a whole new world of music-making by people of my own age. Perhaps this was a defining point in my life and set my resolve to follow a musical career.

The Vienna Boys' Choir visited New Zealand in 1955. I heard them sing in Wellington, not Nelson, and it made a huge impression because it took me beyond the world of brass bands. It provided some relief from the wide, wobbling vibrato of the conically bored euphonium, or 'brass cello' as it was sometimes called. They sang Haydn, Schubert and Mozart ('Schlafe, mein Prinzchen' and the 'Alphabet Song') as well as folk songs such as 'Es wollt ein Jägerlein jagen' and 'O Tannenbaum', and finished up with waltzes by Johann Strauss – *Tales from the Vienna Woods* and *The Blue Danube Waltz.*

But my life was not devoted only to music. The common boyhood country pursuits were another part of it. At the age of 15 I became the New Zealand schoolboy small-bore rifle champion. I was sent to England to shoot for the Lady Gwendolen Guinness prize for boys. I travelled 12,000 miles to fire 12 shots, was beaten for the prize by one point and returned home. This experience kindled within me the desire to travel and confront the wider world. It also flamed my determination always to find the target.

At Wellington College I was put into the Air Training Corps (ATC). This was where all the dregs and riff-raff of the school were placed. We were herded around like sheep and marched about in silly, rough and ill-fitting uniforms. Some teachers and senior boys with hairy legs enjoyed strutting to and fro playing at being soldiers. They relished the chance to bark out orders to make us shape up and fall in. Once we were given guns for shooting practice. My experience of using a rifle is limited to that one occasion. We were shown the parts of the rifle, how to clean it, and given strict rules about handling the weapon. In class we learnt the poem 'Naming of Parts' written in 1942 by Henry Reed, which begins:

Today we have naming of parts. Yesterday,
We had daily cleaning. And tomorrow morning,
We shall have what to do after firing. But today,
Today we have naming of parts. Japonica
Glistens like coral in all of the neighbouring gardens,
And today we have naming of parts.[3]

We were given a gun each and six bullets, which we were to fire at a target. Once all the firing finished we were commanded to go and look at our targets. Mine was completely blank, but the target to my right had a few bullseyes and rather more than six hits. I was not an aspirant for the Lady Gwendolen Guinness Prize.

Among other things Lady Gwendolen Guinness and her husband Rupert Guinness, 2nd Earl of Iveagh, devoted their lives to demonstrating that 'Guinness is good for you'. Lady Gwendolen was the daughter of William Onslow, 4th Earl of Onslow – a somewhat unpopular Governor of New Zealand from 1889 to 1892 and a British Conservative Party politician.

Early in the twentieth century Adam and Charles Black published a series of books called *Peeps at Many Lands*. The New Zealand edition was written by P.A. Vaile and published in 1909. I came across the reference to the Lady Gwendolen Guinness Prize in this book.

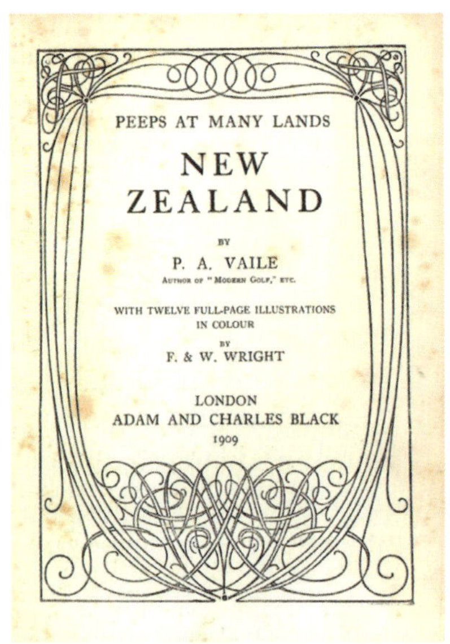

PEEPS AT MANY LANDS

NEW ZEALAND

BY

P. A. VAILE

AUTHOR OF "MODERN GOLF," ETC.

WITH TWELVE FULL-PAGE ILLUSTRATIONS IN COLOUR

BY

F. & W. WRIGHT

LONDON
ADAM AND CHARLES BLACK
1909

Vaile writes:

> A short time ago I went down to Tilbury to meet an Auckland lad of fifteen years of age. He had come 'home' to shoot for the Lady Gwendolen Guinness prize for boys. Some weeks later I went down to Bisley, and saw him shoot. He had come fourteen thousand miles to fire fourteen shots! He was beaten in the Guinness prize by one point. In the afternoon he was beaten again, this time in the miniature rifle competition, by one point. This speaks for itself in many ways. The competition really was too short. Imagine anyone coming fourteen thousand miles to fire fourteen shots! This surely should be obvious to those well-intentioned and zealous persons who attend to and organise these boys' competitions. The test should be made more exhaustive.

On 15 August 1908 15-year-old William Friar, a Colour-Sergeant in the Onehunga High School Cadets, competed at Bisley in Surrey for the Lady Gwendoline Guinness Cup. He was reckoned to be the best schoolboy shooter in New Zealand. At the competition he scored 61 out of 70 points to tie in second place with F. W. Chandler. The cup was won by Ernest Barltrop with 62 points. Friar was wounded at Passchendaele and died on Monday 5 November 1917.

Later in his book Vaile writes:

> Compared with his English brother, the New Zealand workman lives the life of a gentleman – and is one. His skin is clearer and his eye is brighter. He slings his shoulders over his hips, and carries his chest in front of his shoulders.

I have never tried to emulate this elegant posture.

After some years of study at university I worked as a postman, hospital theatre porter and gardener, all the time nurturing an obsession with writing music. I made my way to Europe and set out on the path towards self-sufficiency as a composer.

This is true.

Piero Casadei

Chapter 2
Sunday 13 October 1944

> The composers also wrestled with angels by night and day, but surely they had kindlier adversaries, who, when they succumbed, embraced and were reconciled.
>
> *Rebecca West,* The Fountain Overflows

I was born on Sunday 13 October 1944 in the Salvation Army hospital for unmarried mothers in Wellington. I was probably the only child of both Jack Cresswell and Muriel Sharp. My two older siblings were of uncertain parentage.

Jack was a petty criminal and trickster spending short but frequent stretches of time at Mt Crawford prison. He was well-versed in the repertoire of bawdy and sentimental songs, which he sang with a rasping but curiously doleful voice. Muriel worked odd hours at The Purple Onion, then in its hey-day as Wellington's notorious downtown nightclub. We were never told what she did there – only that it was her place of work. The relationship between my mother and father was stormy.

Moments of great tenderness were too often overshadowed by flashes of ugliness and violence. I found respite from family life only at Karori West Primary School where there was a caring staff and a kindly headmaster, Mr Boon. Mr Boon was deeply involved in the brass band world and taught me to play the trumpet but, along with other boys, I admired him most for the white-walled tyres on his blue Chevrolet. It was however the wild recorder playing and astute teaching of Miss McClintock that aroused my first genuine interest in music. Miss McClintock, tall and elegant, threw her prodigious and selfless energy into training the school choir. This comprised all girls – and me. Perhaps the most poignant experience of my childhood was the choir's Christmas visit to Mt Crawford prison.

Along with 17 girls I sang 'The Holly and the Ivy' to my father and his tearful colleagues. This was the moment I discovered the potency of music and its capacity to move people.

Secondary school was a disaster. I loathed the school and the feeling was reciprocated. The only escape was to follow in my father's footsteps. I ran away and pilfered my passage to San Francisco. There I quickly embraced a more alluring and unrestrained lifestyle. The only possession I carried was a trumpet. Ever since the days of Mr Boon I found some comfort in this instrument. Now it also proved a useful tool.

I loitered my way across America through a succession of free-spirited communities to Toronto's Yorkville Village – a centre of hippiedom and a haven for American draft-dodgers. There I flourished in the city's musical underworld and even appeared briefly, clutching my trumpet, in the definitive rock movie *Woodstock*. But a nasty disagreement with Bud Hill – a trombone player, who also happened to control the local drug traffic – made me flee the country in fear of my life. I crossed the Atlantic and sought out the most northerly university in Britain. With dubiously obtained qualifications I enrolled in Aberdeen as a post-graduate music student and married the daughter of a drainage engineer.

I was born on Sunday 13 October 1944 in the Salvation Army hospital for unmarried mothers in Wellington. I was probably the only child of both Jack Cresswell and Muriel Sharp. My two older siblings were of uncertain parentage.

There is no question that Max and Roger were the children of Jack and Muriel, and I was certainly their third son. They were married in a Salvation Army wedding in 1935. Muriel Sharp became Muriel Cresswell.

My parents' wedding at the Wellington South Salvation Army, December 1935.

Jack was a petty criminal and trickster spending short but frequent stretches of time at Mt Crawford prison. He was well-versed in the repertoire of bawdy and sentimental songs, which he sang with a rasping but curiously doleful voice.

My father was a law-abiding, correct and self-contained man. He was a gentleman – principled, upright, honest, moral, chivalrous and well-mannered. He did not sing bawdy songs and was not sent to prison. A vulgar word was never heard to pass his lips and we could never tell what, if any, risqué thoughts might have crossed his mind. It was always hard to know what he really thought. He was a quiet man with quiet opinions. Everything he did was quiet. He was quietly happy and quietly sad, he spoke quietly, he laughed quietly, he sang quietly, he read quietly, he drove, worked, travelled, slept, got angry and believed quietly, and he loved us quietly. He taught me to play chess and to say, 'Your brother Bob owes my brother Bob a bob. If your brother Bob doesn't give my brother Bob the bob that your brother Bob owes my brother Bob, my brother Bob'll give your brother Bob a bob in the eye.'

My father, Jack Cresswell, 1935.

The Gisborne Community Arts Council commissioned me to write a work to be performed by the New Zealand Symphony Orchestra in 1983 to commemorate the centenary of the arrival of the Salvation Army in New Zealand. The moving spirit behind the commission was Ian Dunsmore, a Gisborne sports retailer, Salvationist, and a founder of the Gisborne International Music Competition.

The Salvation Army 'opened fire' with indoor meetings and a street meeting at the fountain in Dunedin on 1 April 1883. Two 20-year-olds, Captain George Pollard and Lieutenant Edward Wright, were sent to rescue perishing souls. They were met with a mixture of fervid support and merciless ridicule suggesting that the land did not need more pests sent from 'the old country'.

Salvationists were exhorted by William Booth to take up musical instruments to attract people to his meetings. He saw the bass drum as fulfilling a role similar to that of the church bell and made this general rule for the bands in 1884:

> They are to work for the salvation of souls, and for nothing else. We are not going to stick them up on the platform, nor march them through the streets for them to perform and be admired. They are to go there and blow what they are told, and what the commanding officer thinks will be best for the salvation of souls, and if they won't blow for this object, let them stop playing. The man must blow his cornet and shut his eyes, and believe while he plays that he is blowing salvation into somebody.

In a review of a Salvation Army band festival at Clapton Congress Hall on 7 December 1905, George Bernard Shaw wrote:

> It is not enough for a Salvation Army band to play one of its scores technically well. You have only to hand the band parts to Mr Sousa's band or the band of the Grenadier Guards and they will play it equally well. But there should be an emotional difference. It should be possible for a blindfold critic to say which was the Salvation Army band and which was the professional.

Hitchcock's 1935 classic *The 39 Steps* contains the best portrayal of a Salvation Army band in film. With a thudding bass drum a real Salvation Army band marches along playing 'In the Sweet By-and-By'.

The music of the Salvation Army and the message it carries is immediate. The challenge in fulfilling the commission was how to reflect this in a work for symphony orchestra. The title of my work *O!* refers to a popular Salvation Army song with words by William Booth, 'O boundless salvation'. This and another favourite tune, 'Are you washed in the blood of the lamb?', are treated in various ways throughout the piece. The first performances were played in a programme that included Tchaikovsky's *1812 Overture* with orchestra, brass band, cannons and fireworks.

The last conversation of any length that I had with my father involved talking through the score of *O!*, showing him how I had used the various quotations, suggesting things to look for in the music and trying to explain how I had gone about writing it. Sometimes when I was a child I asked him to play simple little piano pieces I had written. On one occasion I gave him something that was meant to have an oom-pah oom-pah accompaniment in the left hand, but I had written it as pah-oom pah-oom. I was upset with myself and wanted to change it, but he said, 'No, leave it, it's more interesting that way.' This was my first lesson in composition, and the only one he ever gave me. He died in 1986 after a blood clot developed following an operation.

Muriel worked odd hours at the Purple Onion, then in its hey-day as Wellington's notorious downtown nightclub. We were never told what she did there – only that it was her place of work. The relationship between my mother and father was stormy.

The Purple Onion opened in Wellington's red light quarter in the 1960s as a strip club and became a hub for drag queens. By this time my mother was probably past the age one would expect of those working in a strip club. In any case she wouldn't have been seen dead near such a place. I can imagine her throwing her hands up in horror at the mere suggestion of its existence. One year, driving north for the summer holiday we stopped outside a hotel in Waiouru, or perhaps Tūrangi, for my father to go into a shop across the road. While we were waiting in the car I said something to my mother about a 'lady' coming out of the hotel bar. She turned to me and said, 'Ladies don't go into hotels, women do' – but she was kind to the alcoholic who lived along the road and among other things took her a Christmas present every year.

My mother, Muriel Sharp, 1931.

Moments of great tenderness were too often overshadowed by flashes of ugliness and violence.

The relationship between my parents was stable and undemonstrative. There was never any sign of intimacy and only rarely were there moments of conflict or tension. It was not an unhappy marriage, but it is difficult to know just how happy it was. Max remembers once hearing my father mumble under his breath, 'Jack be nimble, Jack be quick.'

My mother died in 1982. She suffered from emphysema and her mind had become a little disorientated. She was not happy in the years after her three sons left home and very gradually became less rational. When it was suggested that she be taken into hospital to give my father some respite she faded and died.

I found respite from family life only at Karori West Primary School where there was a caring staff and a kindly headmaster, Mr Boon. Mr Boon was deeply involved in the brass band world and taught me to play the trumpet but, along with other boys, I admired him most for the white-walled tyres on his blue Chevrolet.

We lived in a typical 1940s state house in a friendly neighbourhood at 30 Victory Avenue. There was a lovely view of Karori Park and the hills on the other side of the Makara Road. Housewives would call 'cooee' to each other and gossip over the fence. We were impressed when a neighbour, Mr Stone, showed off a new shiny black portable radio that started when you opened the lid. Further up the road on the other side lived a man who was said to keep his coal in the bath. Another neighbour, Mr Cartwright, always unleashed a sumptuous display of fireworks on Guy Fawkes night. His roman candles were bigger than our roman candles, his Mount Vesuvius's erupted with a blaze of colour, ours went 'pfssst', his Tom Thumbs went 'thwack', ours went 'pop', his jumping jacks gleefully leapt while ours staggered and jerked, and his sky rockets nearly took out the moon.

The milkman used to make his deliveries early in the morning. My grandparents in Kilbirnie still had theirs brought by horse and cart – we were not so lucky. At night we put out the milk bottles with tokens in them and one year thieves went about pilfering them. The local policeman, known as 'swivel head' because he was always looking the other way, was summoned. His advice was simply to 'watch them in the holidays'.

I had a friend who lived just along the road. When it came time for us to start school I was told that he had gone to the convent school. I never saw him again. On my first day my mother took me down on the school bus, which ran from the top of the hill to Karori West Primary School. After school she came down in the bus to take me home. As soon as we got on I ran to sit at the back on my own while she took her seat at the front. She never took me to school again.

At 30 Victory Avenue, ready for my first day at Karori West Primary School, February 1950.

The first task I was given at school was to fill two milk bottles with water to clean up after a child who had been afraid to ask to go to the toilet. Water play, the sand pit, building blocks, the alphabet, *Janet and John*[1] and the times tables were all part of the school day, but my favourite activities were painting with messy watercolours, scribbling on paper with crayons or making chalk drawings on the blackboard.

When I was six I drew a Salvation Army band.

Karori West Primary School became Karori West Normal School the year after I left. Mr Boon was the headmaster in 1955. As far as I know he had no involvement in the brass band world and he did not teach me to play the trumpet – my father did that – but my first brass instrument was the E-flat tenor horn. Mr Boon had a blue car with white walled tyres, but I don't know if it was a Chevrolet. It might have been a Wolseley, or a Holden or an Oldsmobile.

Mr Boon enthusiastically supported a campaign run by the Department of Health to encourage healthy eating and teeth cleaning. Posters were pasted around the school calling for us to 'kill Bertie the Germ of tooth decay' and, in the style of the artist Arcimboldi, to be healthy kiwis.

New Zealand Railways Publicity Branch and R E Owen. Ref: Eph-C-DENTAL-1950s-02. Alexander Turnbull Library

New Zealand Department of Health. Ref: Eph-D-HEALTH-NZDH-1950S-03.
Alexander Turnbull Library

Our dentist Mr Somerville had been a keen boxer. He made an impression of my teeth when I was seven.

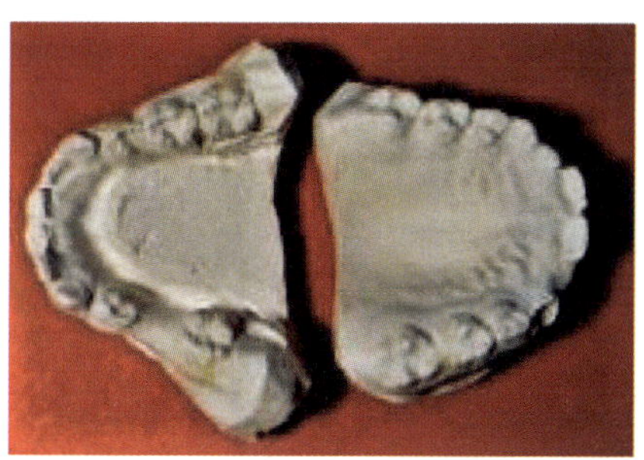

It was however the wild recorder playing and astute teaching of Miss McClintock that aroused my first genuine interest in music. Miss McClintock, tall and elegant, threw her prodigious and selfless energy into training the school choir. This comprised all girls – and me.

Miss McClintock took the choir in which I was the only boy, but I did not see or hear her play the recorder. Every year we took part in the Wellington Primary School Choir Festival conducted by Harry Botham. Before the annual concert we were taken during school time to the Wellington Town Hall for a rehearsal. Once as we were preparing to leave, the teacher Mr Barrett said, 'Off you go girls – and boy.'

We sang such things as the duet from *Don Giovanni* 'La ci darem la mano', translated as 'hand linked in hand we wander', 'Where'er You Walk', 'The Ash Grove', 'Funiculi Funicula', 'The Skye Boat Song', 'Pōkarekare Ana' and 'Aotearoa' – a song written by H. Temple White in honour of the royal visit in 1953–54. My contribution to the choir was ineffectual, but I was enchanted by all this music.

Karori Stream, which flows from the hills of South Karori into Cook Strait, runs close beside the school. Native vegetation lines its banks, an array of native fish swim in it and from time to time we were taken there for nature study classes. Once a new young teacher took us and when we reached the stream she suddenly whipped off her skirt to reveal a pair of shorts all ready for wading and small boys gasped.

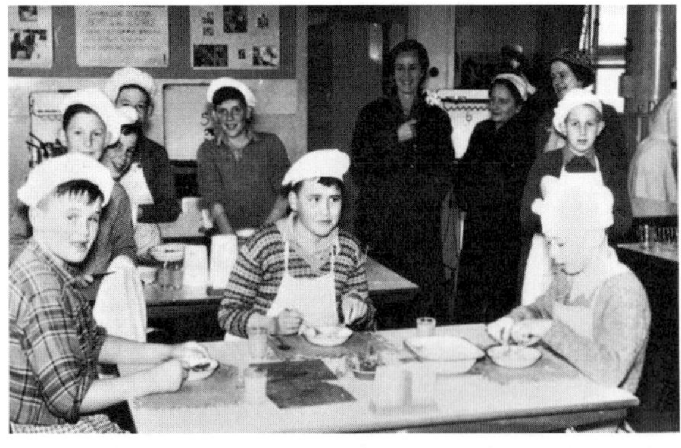

Our 1957 cooking class: I am in the centre with Terry Kerse on my right and Trevor Philips on my left.

One morning a week we had woodwork with Mr Brains, while the girls had cooking with Mrs Hewson. My attempts at woodwork resulted in a misshapen wooden spoon and a rather unstable coffee table. In the second term of 1957, my last year at primary school, the girls were given a term of woodwork and the boys a term of cooking. This was much more to my taste. Two recipes I particularly remember making were an unpalatable tomato soup made with milk, and the more appetising cheese and bacon on toast.

Perhaps the most poignant experience of my childhood was the choir's Christmas visit to Mt Crawford prison. Along with 17 girls I sang 'The Holly and the Ivy' to my father and his tearful colleagues. This was the moment I discovered the potency of music and its capacity to move people.

Mt Crawford and Crawford Road were named after James Coutts Crawford, a Scot who arrived in New Zealand in 1839, settled in Wellington and acquired the land that became the suburb of Miramar. Among other things Crawford was a naval officer, a member of the geological societies of London, Vienna and Edinburgh, president of the Wellington Philosophical Society, a farmer, an explorer, a magistrate and a public servant. He ran a butchery company, built a tunnel, kept a sketchbook and painted watercolours. He named the suburb of Kilbirnie after the small town in Scotland 44 miles from his birthplace in Strathaven.

Our maternal grandparents lived at 9 Crawford Road, Kilbirnie. They had an attractive early twentieth century house with a splendid view over Evans Bay and lovely ball finials. In the late 1950s the house was mangled by renovations and the view somewhat spoiled by the reclamation of land for the construction of Wellington Airport. We moved from Victory Avenue to Henry Street, Kilbirnie, in 1959. The view across Kilbirnie Park, Evans Bay and up to Mt Crawford Prison evoked visions of escaped prisoners roaming the hill at night.

In the early 1960s I joined the choir of All Saints Anglican Church, Hataitai. From time to time the choir visited the prison to sing hymns and carols. 'The Holly and the Ivy' would have had particular resonance for my father if he had been a prisoner – his sister was called Ivy. For one of the church festivals a prisoner with a rich baritone voice was let out to sing with the choir. After the festivities he absconded.

Secondary school was a disaster. I loathed the school and the feeling was reciprocated.

When I started at Wellington College I had great expectations. These were quickly dispelled and before long I became bored and disenchanted. I was bewildered by the sight of schoolmasters wearing black gowns gone green with grime and spattered with white chalk dust. The teaching was lacklustre, the ethos insensitive, the classes tedious, the textbooks time-worn and dog-eared, the drinking fountains dubious, the corridors filled with short-trousered galoots, the library fusty, the tuck-shop grotty, the door knobs sticky, the music stands wonky and the medicine balls flabby. The classrooms were clammy, and the teachers cranky and addled after lunch. Among the staff prowled the school bullies itching to use the belt on adolescent boys' bottoms. Imagination was suppressed, creativity stifled and the arts looked down on as something morally questionable. This little empire was ruled by a dictatorial and boorish headmaster. Looking back at those days is like observing the life of a completely different person. Those who rhapsodise about their school days must have led very dull lives thereafter.

When a teacher at another school wrote on a child's report 'faculties dormant' the angry parent came to the parent–teacher evening, grabbed him by the collar and said, 'How dare you call my son a fucking doormat.' My school career was something like that. I went on strike, refused to study or do any homework and withdrew into my own fanciful world to become a mental truant with dormant faculties. Growing up was a struggle against churlish and hostile forces.

There were just two good things about the school day – the rousing massed hymn singing first thing at morning assembly and the 3.30pm bell. The one tiny glimmer of hope was in music. The music master Mr Radford was a good musician with a soul-destroying job. Once a week we had a 40-minute period belting out songs like 'On the Road to Mandalay', 'Blow the Wind Southerly', 'Trade Winds' ('The squeaking fiddle, and the soughing in the sail'), 'The Mermaid' ('And the land-lubbers lying down below, below, below') and John Masefield's 'Captain Stratton's Fancy', with these particularly memorable verses to delight schoolboys set to music by Peter Warlock.

Oh some are fond of red wine, and some are fond of white,
And some are all for dancing by the pale moonlight;
But rum alone's the tipple, and the heart's delight
Of the old bold mate of Henry Morgan.

Oh some are fond of fiddles, and a song well sung,
And some are all for music for to lilt upon the tongue;
But mouths were made for tankards, and for sucking at the bung,
Says the old bold mate of Henry Morgan.[2]

The only encouraging thing that was ever said to me at the school came from Mr Radford. It was a small, but for me, significant and perceptive remark. I wrote some music for the school orchestra, which I took to show him as it progressed. He took my appalling and naïve attempts seriously and told me that I had a 'good sense of instrumentation'.

The only escape was to follow in my father's footsteps. I ran away and pilfered my passage to San Francisco. There I quickly embraced a more alluring and unrestrained lifestyle. The only possession I carried was a trumpet. Ever since the days of Mr Boon I found some comfort in this instrument. Now it also proved a useful tool.

There are moth caterpillars that burrow into the ground and stay there until they emerge as grown-up moths. Only after I surfaced as a student at Victoria University of Wellington did I reach a tolerable level of consciousness. I began studying for a Bachelor of Music degree. David Farquhar and Douglas Lilburn, two of New Zealand's most prominent composers, were on the staff, so it was the right place for me. I studied for the Bachelor of Music degree between 1965 and 1967, and in 1968 took the extra honours year.

In those days there were no dead New Zealand composers. Lilburn's position was unique; he had no local models and was the first significant composer to be formed in the country. He did not teach composition. The nearest he came to it was in the orchestration classes where he set increasingly challenging piano pieces for us to try our hand at, culminating in the honours class in a very complex piece by the German composer Giselher Klebe.[3] In these tutorials we were able to have a good exchange of views because he was intrigued

Playing the Common Room piano in the Music Department, 1967. Robert Carew

by some of my solutions. A convincing orchestration depends on understanding how the music is constructed and what it might be trying to convey. The lessons were just as much in analysis and composition as in orchestration.

Apart from the orchestration tutorials my relationship with him was awkward. There seemed to be a mutual wariness. Lilburn's classes throughout the four years were always very formal; we were Mr Cresswell, Miss Kerr, Miss Shorter, Mr James and so on. His counterpoint tutorials were unremarkable and his acoustics lectures dry. He was never relaxed when teaching. His nervousness was noticeable in lectures as he lit up one cigarette to keep between his fingers while another lay smouldering in an ashtray on the piano. Our sensibilities were somewhat different. I was struck when Dobbs Franks conducted the first raucous performance in New Zealand of *Octandre* by Edgard Varèse, but Douglas dismissed it as a 'collection of raspberries'.

For the capping procession of 1968, which celebrated those who finished their degrees in 1967, we formed a band with a motley collection of woodwind and brass instruments. 'Sergeant Pepper's Lonely Tarts' led the procession through the streets of Wellington

Preparing for the 1968 capping procession.

Robyn Boyes and Catherine Mawson hold placards, an unidentified person looks at the camera and Robert Carew plays the saxophone. I am on the right.

with a couple of Sousa marches. Afterwards we hurried up the hill to the music department, where a lunchtime concert was just finishing. As soon as the applause died down we struck up with 'The Stars and Stripes'. The door opened immediately, and there was Douglas with a pink smiling face beckoning us in and clapping in time to the music. I had never seen him in such an unbuttoned state.

Years later, visiting Douglas in his Ascot Terrace house in Thorndon, we were much more relaxed – especially after a glass of wine, sitting on opposite sides of the room and chatting happily. The New Zealand Symphony Orchestra performed my cello concerto with Ross Pople in 1987. By that time Douglas had stopped going to concerts, but he came to the rehearsal in the Michael Fowler Centre and sat upstairs. After the rehearsal Catherine met him coming down the stairs with tears in his eyes. He said to her, 'That was beautiful. I could never have written anything like that.'

Singing in the university choir, the Bach Choir of Wellington and the choir of St Peter's Church, all under the direction of Anthony Jennings, was one of the delights throughout these student days. We sang mostly Bach and Handel in the bigger choirs, and concentrated on sixteenth-century composers such as Palestrina, Byrd and Victoria in the church choir.

The university choir rehearsing Handel's Dixit Dominus *– I am hiding behind my score with the trio at the back, 1967.* Robert Carew

With Anthony Jennings at my graduation, 1968.

In the counterpoint class of 1966, taken by Margaret Nielsen,[4] we were given Latin texts to set in the style of these composers. The challenge of devising interweaving lines that made sense both harmonically and melodically was utterly engrossing. The value of these skills, the study of four-part harmony in the style of J. S. Bach and of various serial techniques, should not be underestimated. All the methods I have concocted for my own use derive from these disciplines.

The influence of Bartók and Stravinsky is clear in some of my early work. A trio for clarinet, violin and piano written in 1967 drew on Bartók's *Contrasts*, but was based on a 12-note row. The students for the first performances were Robert Carew (clarinet), John North (violin) and Bruce Greenfield (piano). A couple of years later Margaret Nielsen and two players from the New Zealand

Douglas Lilburn.
From the Douglas Lilburn Collection, Alexander Turnbull Library. ATL Ref: PAColl-7737-3-03

Margaret Nielsen holding Lilburn's Four Preludes, *1989.*
Music in New Zealand

David Farquhar (1928–2007) with Margaret Nielsen (1933–2023) after a Music Department concert in the Hunter Building, 1977.
Te Herenga Waka – Victoria University of Wellington

Symphony Orchestra recorded it for Radio New Zealand. By then my work had moved on and I felt diffident about it, but Margaret was reassuring and appreciative. After a recital of my piano music by Stephen De Pledge in Wellington in 2007, she told me that listening to my piano music made her think about harmony differently.

David Farquhar took the honours composition class in 1968. To be encouraged but left to my own devices was all I was looking for and David did just that. Each week we took our efforts along, sat at the piano and mulled them over through a cloud of his cigarillo smoke. There were no exercises to do, just a few suggestions made and one or two questions asked, but otherwise just gentle support.

Any fellow student was liable to be dragooned into playing my music. Fortunately most of these scores are lost, although there is always the danger that they may be lurking in a cupboard somewhere. Among other things there were some outlandish 'cantatas' with absurdist libretti and hybrid casts of speakers, actors, singers, instrumentalists and exploding rubbish bins.

Sir Granville Ransome Bantock (1868–1946) was a prolific English composer of music in all genres, including a music hall song, 'Who'll give a penny to the monkey'. None of us knew anything of his music, but we used the centenary of his birth to present a concert

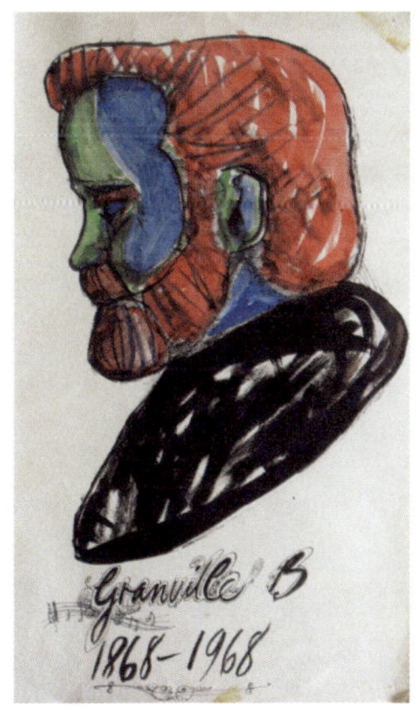

Posters for the Granville Bantock Festival designed by Richard N. Russell. Richard was the best man at our wedding in 1972.

of disparate and inappropriate music. The programme included a short piano piece by Bantock called 'Long Live Canadian Maidens' from his *Sixty Patriotic Songs*, a cantata *Bacchus in India,* which I devised, and *Fire! Fire!* – a 'descriptive fantasia' by Ezra Read, an Englishman six years older than Bantock, who was a bandmaster in the Boer War. He wrote easy piano pieces and patriotic marches. With great verve Elizabeth Kerr declaimed a commentary put together from annotations in the score, while I played the piano.

The honours class of 1968 comprised five students – Elizabeth Kerr, Gordon Burt, Ian Harris, Denis Smalley and myself. It was an unusual year because we all graduated with first-class honours. Jenny McLeod, recently returned from study in Paris, took the analysis class. We analysed Stravinsky's *Le Sacre du Printemps*, Webern's *Konzert Op. 24*, Boulez' *Structures Book 1* and Berio's *Circles*. Sometimes on a Wednesday morning we went to a café in Oriental Bay for the class, but this stopped once the powers that be got wind of it. On the morning of 10 April the Lyttelton to Wellington ferry *Wahine* sank entering Wellington Harbour in a horrendous storm and 53 lives were lost. We received constant updates throughout the class because Gordon Burt's brother was on board – he survived.

With Gordon Burt, Denis Smalley and Ian Harris at graduation, 1969.
Our other classmate, Elizabeth Kerr, did not join us for graduation
as she had already left to teach in Toronto.

After my time in Wellington, Jenny McLeod became professor of music in 1971 so I did not experience her colourful régime. In more recent years, whenever I visited her in her Pukerua Bay eyrie, the sky was always blue and the view of Kapiti Island magnificent. I have arrived wondering what her next enthusiasm might be – musical or mystical, intellectual or spiritual, political or philosophical, cynical or sentimental, teetotal or bibulous. Whatever it may be she is always able to expound it passionately with a remarkably indefinite grip on reality.

With Jenny McLeod at Pukerua Bay, 2006.

John North, violinist and then violist in the New Zealand Broadcasting Corporation Symphony Orchestra took a year's leave to study. He sported a long beard which was frowned upon by the orchestral management. A letter from him some years later captures something of the atmosphere of the time.[5]

18/5/82

Dear Lyell,

I believe you will remember me, a violinist on leave from the N.Z.B.C.S.O. in 1968 and studying full-time at V.U.W..

I heard over the A.B.C. last night a recording of your "Salm", listened to it with enjoyment and great interest. I gathered the recording was of a live performance in N.Z.. The orchestra sounded good – I guess you have heard the recording, if you were not present when it was made. I did not recognize the cello solo playing but presume it was Simenauer. Your work was programmed with a Japanese percussion solo piece written for the woman who played it, the two works having been played at a Paris Rostrum?

Last night's was not the first of your works to have been broadcast here: certainly a violin concerto has been on the air – I don't know if this would have been the recording with Alex Lindsay that I was in; and I have been questioned about you!

The announcer last night gave us the background / inspiration of the piece, and something about you (Utrecht etc.). If you were in fact born in 1944, that was only 4 years after me: whereas in 1968 I had been 9 years in the workforce and felt ridiculously old. "Salm" was a good way distant from the clarinet/violin/piano trio I was in in 1968 (my big tune began)

The announcer gave indirectly the approximate address on this aerogramme.

I'm aware how much I owe to the contact I had with the staff Fred gathered at Victoria and with the students that were attracted to the department – I owe a lot to the old bastard himself. I get to play a good deal of local new music here, generally in chamber ensemble but sometimes in solo. I have been 8 years in the M.S.O. violas rank-and-file, expect to be there till I retire, am happy in it. (Melbourne is my home city.) The orchestra itself is a more felicitous version of what the N.Z.S.O. was in my time; it does a quota of Australian and international contemporary music – I look forward to the first Cresswell work we do (it has never in my time done an N.Z. piece, or maybe a Jon Rimmer). – The most recent performance of a contemporary piece you might know was a horn concerto written for and played by Barry Tuckwell, "Actaeon" by R.R. Bennett.

It is a little risky in these very modern times, and amongst musicians, enquiring after spouses – but if not, my regards to Catherine. I wonder if she plays her cello much. – Equally, you may be a family man. I remain a cast-iron bachelor.

(There is some space left, I could have printed bigger.) From time to time there are forays here from Geoffrey Coker the counter-tenor, the Wellington Baroque Ensemble et al. I believe Tony Jennings is here at the moment. I have often wondered if there was an unusual aggregation of talent and of vivid personalities at Victoria in 1968 – you would be in a position to know, whereas I have done no further degree nor study here. I have not left Australia since returning, and with house-buying and job there's no trip in sight – my life can be nothing like that of the globe-trotting Lyell Cresswell: I rationalize staying at home with waffle about an unadulterated Australasian musicality.

Memory plays tricks; but I believe it was your cyclic orchestral suite unkindly amputated by Dobbs Franks (now living here) at ~~a~~ Universities' Arts Festival in Auckland, have always regretted not speaking out at the last rehearsal – but now it does not matter in the least. Also I remember a mock Analysis lecture from you – theme .

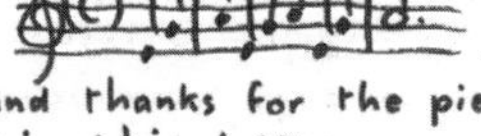

If I may, congratulations on and thanks for the piece last night. – And I have also enjoyed writing this letter.

Jolen Nash

DO NOT WRITE BEYOND THIS LINE

Some say that Professor Frederick Page was an opinionated snob and perhaps there is some truth in this, but it was part of his charm. He had his opinions – Telemann wrote music for 'washing the dishes to', Brahms was 'stodgy and overcooked' – and he enjoyed goading those whose opinions did not accord with his own. Wafting into lectures in his gown he simply dictated notes and, despite an antipathy to recorded music, he occasionally took out a vinyl record, wiped it with his sleeve and played an example, marking the spot with a piece of chalk. A tulip seemed to grow out of his head as he glided up and down stairs – a result of practising the Alexander Technique. The epicentre of the musical avant-garde in those days was the Darmstadt Summer Course,[6] from which he returned in 1958 with a zest for new music that stayed with him for the rest of his life. The enthusiasm that he brought could be indiscriminate, but it was infectious and this, rather than his teaching, was an inspiration. The same could be said of his piano playing. Stockhausen piano pieces and Boulez sonatas were played with flair rather than accuracy.

The following lines from an epitaph for Frederick Prince of Wales, father of George III were given to us to set to music in the final exams one year.

Here lies Fred,
Who was alive and is dead.
Had it been his father,
I had much rather,
But since 'tis only Fred,
Who was alive and is dead,
Why there's no more to be said.

Prince Frederick died after being hit by a cricket ball. One of Fred Page's brothers, Milford Laurenson 'Curly' Page, was captain of the New Zealand cricket team that toured England in 1937, his third tour of England. In 1928 the Wisden Cricketers' Almanack says he, '. . . showed himself a thoroughly capable and consistent batsman'. He also played one game of rugby for the All Blacks in 1928. Fred told me that once he asked his brother how he managed to hit the ball and the reply was 'you watch it'.

Fred was warm in his appreciation of my music. John Mansfield

Thomson[7] told me that Fred wrote to him and said 'Cresswell is the one to watch'. When he died, his wife Eve Page wrote to us to say that Fred died in his armchair with his beloved cat on his lap.

The world beyond musical goings-on involved protests against the war in Vietnam, parties in grubby student flats, earnest conversations in dark coffee bars draped with fishing nets, happenings, poetry readings in the cemetery, anarchic rallies on the roof of the Taj Mahal and all the things we were supposed to do in the 1960s.

I wrote satirical shows for, and performed in the Salvation Army Student Festivals in 1966 and 1967.

Wellington's Taj Mahal was built as a public toilet in 1928–29.

I graduated with a BMusHons in 1969.

I loitered my way across America through a succession of free-spirited communities to Toronto's Yorkville Village – a centre of hippiedom and a haven for American draft-dodgers. There I flourished in the city's musical underworld and even appeared briefly, clutching my trumpet, in the definitive rock movie Woodstock. *But a nasty disagreement with Bud Hill – a trombone player, who also happened to control the local drug traffic – made me flee the country in fear of my life.*

In 1969 I was awarded a Canadian Commonwealth Scholarship to study for a Master of Music degree at Toronto University. The Woodstock festival was held from 15 to 18 August 1969, days before I left Wellington for Toronto. I did not travel with a trumpet. In Toronto I lived in the St George Graduate Student Residence on Bloor Street West, not so far from Yorkville Village, which is now a fashionable shopping district. At the time it was the centre of Canadian hippiedom with a lively nightlife and colourful Bohemian shops. Nearby was Rochdale College, which was described as an 'experiment in counterculture education' and 'North America's largest drug distribution warehouse'.

During the year I acquired a multifarious range of friends. Among them were students, American draft-dodgers objecting to the war in Vietnam, a librarian, an orthodontist and a racing car driver. Charles 'Bud' Hill was not involved in drug trafficking. He was a music teacher in one of the local high schools and had taken a year off teaching for postgraduate study. He and his wife Nancy were very kind to me during my stay. They met in West Germany in the 1950s where Nancy was a dancer and Bud played the trombone in various jazz groups. From time to time we would go to the jazz clubs. Two nights that I remember particularly were when we heard Earl 'Fatha' Hines and Stan Kenton's Jazz Orchestra.

Hines was near the end of his career when we heard him play with his trio in a smoky downtown bar to a handful of listeners. His playing, complemented with little grunts and snatches of singing, was mesmerising. We were able to mingle and chat with him and his inventive drummer, who had a tube attached to one of the drums so that he could blow into it to alter the tension of the skin and raise the pitch, just like the pedal timpani glissando. Gunther Schuller writes:

> Hines's achievements in dramatically extending the role of the piano in jazz – at times tantamount to creating an entirely new conception for it – would be remarkable enough if they encompassed a lifetime. But the startling fact is that Hines radically transformed jazz piano when he was barely 22 years old, expanding upon all previously established piano styles from ragtime to the stride idioms of the early twenties. In Hines's hands the piano's full technical/physical/acoustic resources were brought into play in a manner that was not only new but was not to be approached, let alone surpassed, until decades later in differing ways by Art Tatum, Errol Garner, Bud Powell, and Oscar Peterson.[8]

Stan Kenton and his vibrant and brassy jazz orchestra played in a bigger ballroom. His music was not so fashionable around the time of Woodstock, but the older audience was dressed for the occasion and nostalgically swayed and tapped their feet in time to the music. The men were in light brown, light blue or even yellow suits and two-tone shoes in brown and white, or black and white leather, or blue suede shoes, brown suede shoes, winkle-pickers or various types of creeper. The women wore swing dresses and pencil dresses, or pleated skirts, blouses with puffed sleeves and bright shoes with stiletto heels.

These excursions made a lasting impression on me. Traces of jazz can quite often be found seeping into my work. The influence doesn't come from any specific style, group or person. It is more to do with ideas and techniques of jazz – the displacement of rhythm, the subversion of pulse, the continuity, the way the music breathes and swings and, of course, the harmonies. Improvisation is one of the cornerstones of jazz, but this has no part in my music.

My time at Toronto University was crucial to my musical evolution. I took four courses: ethnomusicology, electronic music, contemporary techniques and composition.

The ethnomusicology class was taken by the eminent ethnomusicologist Mieczyslaw Kolinski. He was a lovely Polish man with moving stories of his escape from the Nazis through Belgium. We spent all the time analysing folksongs using a recondite method that he had devised to correlate the music of different cultures.

The electronic music class was taken by Gustav Ciamaga.[9] These were the days of musique concrète, analogue tape recorders, oscillators, analogue ring modulators, tape splicing, tape loops, manipulating sounds by speeding them up, slowing them down or playing them backwards, and the absorbing search for new sound sources. I enjoyed the tactile nature of it all – the sensual experience of touching the sounds and moving the little pieces of magnetic tape around before assembling them into a composition. Then there was the added frisson of the danger of carefully ordered snippets of tape being blown across the floor when someone opened a door, or speakers erupting at the touch of a knob. Something was lost with the advance of digitalisation and dependence on computer programmers.

This was the first time I had been away from New Zealand. I was nervously taking in a whole new world. My composition teacher John Weinzweig[10] put me at ease right from the start. He was kind, supportive and thought provoking. His method of teaching composition was simple. In the first few weeks he set a few exercises; writing for a solo instrument or small combinations of instruments using a limited pitch range – one, two or three notes – then 12-note canons, word setting, orchestration and so on. He played through the exercises on the piano, pointed out strong points and shortcomings, made suggestions and then asked for some explanation. Very soon I began working on projects of my own and the process was the same – a subtle way of guidance allowing me to find my own way. Of course, as a cocky student I didn't always accept his suggestions and we would argue them through, but he was perceptive and very encouraging. I learned how to discipline my musical thoughts and organise my musical material.

My first orchestral piece, *Concerto for violin and orchestra,* was written as part of my degree. It follows the traditional three-movement fast–slow–fast pattern, but has a cadenza in the second movement. In each movement a different section of the orchestra is set in contrast with the violin: in the first movement woodwind; second movement percussion; and third movement brass, with the strings holding things together throughout. The music is based loosely on two symmetrical 12-note rows, one for the soloist and one for the orchestra. They are related like this: soloist 1 2 3 4 5 6 7 8 9 10 11 12 and orchestra: 1 3 5 7 9 11 2 4 6 8 10 12.

Soloist:

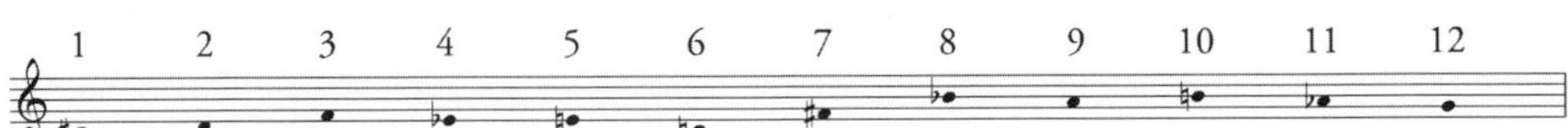

Minor 2nd, Minor 3rd, Major 2nd, Minor 2nd, Major 3rd, Augmented 4th, Major 3rd, Minor 2nd, Major 2nd, Minor 3rd, Minor 2nd

Orchestra:

1 3 5 7 9 11 2 4 6 8 10 12

Major 3rd, Minor 2nd, Major 2nd, Minor 3rd, Minor 2nd, Augmented 4th, Minor 2nd, Minor 3rd, Major 2nd (Minor 7th), Minor 2nd, Major 3rd

Each week as I was writing the concerto, I would take it along to show John and account for all I had written. These long sessions were very helpful, but there was one thing I found rather irksome. He was an inveterate pipe smoker and his small room reeked of a particularly strong tobacco. I always emerged feeling somewhat queasy – not from the effect of concentrating on the music.

In Toronto I drew this cellist for Catherine.

I crossed the Atlantic and sought out the most northerly university in Britain. With dubiously obtained qualifications I enrolled in Aberdeen as a post-graduate music student . . .

When my year in Toronto was up I flew to London and spent three months at the end of 1969 hitchhiking around Britain and Europe. I saw a lot and came across interesting people, but it was a largely solitary experience. I never knew where I might end up for the night.

In Hamburg I fell in with an earnest student called Klaus who warned me against pickpockets and the wild women of the notorious Reeperbahn district, then in its prime. On the night train through East Germany to Berlin I shared a compartment with a German girl who made the uncanny prediction that the wall would come down in 20 years. Both East and West Berlin were full of signs of World War II. It felt uncomfortably close. Crossing the checkpoint the East German guard took my camera, looked at it, said 'mm Kodak' and gave it back to me.

I stumbled across a couple of Australians in Paris intent on finding Vegemite. I was looking for Picasso's first studios in rue Gabrielle, Montmartre and down the road at Le Bateau-Lavoir. At the Louvre I gazed on the Mona Lisa's smile and was followed around by her penetrating eyes. In those days it was possible to spend decent time looking, unencumbered by hordes of tourists with cameras and elbows. I shared rough Algerian red wine, toenails and all, with locals in a small café while listening rapt to a soulful accordionist, and drank superior French wine with a chance acquaintance in the art deco surroundings of La Coupole brasserie.

With meticulous planning, no mobile phones, no email and no internet, I met Andrea at the magnificent, megalithic railway station in Milan. I knew him in Toronto where he was studying statistics. We ate risotto alla milanese in a lovely osteria and went to the Dominican monastery of Santa Maria delle Grazie to spend time worshipping Leonardo's 'Last Supper', then in bad repair – once again without a crowd of tourists.

I had never seen so many soldiers, guns, tanks, checkpoints, roadblocks, broken windows, piles of rubble, street murals and frightened people as I saw in Belfast. In Fishguard I met a rabid Welsh nationalist, and in Scotland I was picked up by a man driving all 700 miles from the south coast of England to John O'Groats in one day to see the northern lights. In London a strike by dustmen left great piles of rubbish everywhere. The Conservative government had just lifted an embargo on trade with South Africa and I joined a protest in Downing Street. Earlier in the year a tour by the South African cricket team had been abandoned. In October I hitched my way to Exeter to hear Rostropovich and the Bournemouth Symphony Orchestra give the second performance of Lutosławski's wonderful cello concerto.

On my way back to New Zealand in November 1970 I stopped in Tel Aviv. The military presence in Jerusalem was even greater and more disquieting than Belfast. I walked past two Arab gentlemen standing at an ancient city gate. One of them pointed at me and the other shook his head. What if he had nodded?

At the beginning of 1971 I moved to Dunedin – where Catherine was in her final year as a student at Otago University – and joined the staff at Taieri High School. My career as a secondary school music teacher lasted about three months. Those were the days of long hair and big flower-power ties, which displeased the ex-RNZAF headmaster rather more than the children, and it seemed that I was told off more often than most of them. Since I was not a trained teacher, I was soon replaced by a real one. Later I was told that the staff had a bet that my hair would soon be cut. It was not. The teaching I most enjoyed was a third form English class. One day I put a lettuce on the table and asked the pupils to write about it. There were some imaginative responses – one essay began with the words, 'The lettuce looks like Mr Cresswell's hair.' Another essay, on 'The High Spots of Mosgiel' brought references to 'the mill chiminey' and 'the boiling green'. Near the end I was asked to supervise a girls' hockey team. Fortunately this did not come about.

The Song Book from 1969 proudly displays the school motto, 'Esse quam videri',[11] taken from Cicero's essay *De Amicitia*. The book contains hymns, wholesome songs and the Taieri High School song – Number 124.

Here's to Taieri High School
Give a cheer, give a cheer.
Here's to Taieri High School
Give a cheer, give a cheer.
We'll learn and we'll remember,
From February to December,
So here's to Taieri High School
Give a cheer.

Working for the New Zealand Post Office had supported me in school holidays and through my student days in Wellington, so I turned to it again and became a postman in Dunedin. I was efficient and conscientious. It was in my own interest to finish my round as quickly as possible in order to get on with other things, but I have to say that very little of the music I wrote then has been allowed to survive.

One howling, windy day as I was making my way around the Belleknowes run, an aerogramme flew from my hands and swirled away vanishing into the great beyond. I felt helpless and guilty, and next morning reported the loss to the supervisor. I wondered if this loss meant that lives were blighted, love affairs doomed, dreams dashed, or tidings of comfort and joy held back. On the other hand friendships might have been saved, offence not taken, insults blown away, or perhaps the letter found its destination after being discovered in a blocked drain, a compost heap or nestled in a cabbage patch.

Those of us who were keen to get on with other activities during the day would line up early every morning outside the door waiting to be let in to start work sorting the mail for our own run. Among the general sorters there was a long-faced and taciturn curmudgeon called Tom, who would grumble bad-temperedly whenever we came to take our share of the mail.

As well as writing music I flirted with painting and thought of calling all my paintings 'Tom'.

'Tom' 1972, acrylic on hardboard.

When I left the job to go abroad and further my studies I was told that I could take a year's leave from the Post Office and then return to the job. Perhaps if I'd taken their advice I would have risen to the heights of Postmaster General, had a big house and been much better off than surviving all these years as a freelance composer.

In the winter of 1971 my parents came down to stay in the nice little flat I had in Lachlan Avenue. Since they were of good Salvation Army stock they were strict teetotallers. One sunny Sunday afternoon during their visit, the composer Anthony Watson[12] and his partner, Cynthia Greensill dropped in for a chat, bringing some bottles of beer. I spent an excruciating afternoon being polite and pretending that there was no beer sitting there. At one point Tony said he had heard the Salvation Army band playing outside that morning and joked about the trombones playing with vibrato. This must have made my parents particularly nervous – to think that a trombone with vibrato might be more evil than the demon drink had never occurred to them.

. . . and married the daughter of a drainage engineer.

Catherine and I were married at St Ninian's Presbyterian Church, Karori on 4 January 1972. Her father Keith Mawson, as Wellington's drainage engineer, kept the city's drains and sewers flowing for years. When travelling abroad he delighted in visiting sewage treatment plants.

Catherine and the drainage engineer waiting to walk down the aisle – I composed the music for our wedding; a bagpipe solo accompanied Catherine's entrance.

The wedding party – Sylvia Cresswell held by Roger Cresswell, Wendy Albiston Cresswell, Jack Cresswell, Catherine, me, Muriel Sharp Cresswell, Max Cresswell, Mary Cresswell and Miriam Meyerhoff.

Chapter 3
Monday 13 October 1944

> I frankly confess, that in executing many of the Drawings, my Pencil has but faintly copied out those Images that my Fancy suggested, and had they not been published till I could have pronounced them perfect, perhaps they had never seen the Light. Nevertheless, I was not upon that Account afraid to let them go abroad, for I have been told, that the greatest Masters of every other Art have laboured under the same difficulty.
>
> *Thomas Chippendale, preface to*
> The Gentleman & Cabinet Maker's Director

Marquetry and Parquetry have always played an important role in my life. They have been both mother and father to me.

My grandfather Henry Proctor Sharp came from a long line of Yorkshire coracle makers. His dream was to build a coracle capable of taking him single-handedly to a new life in America. This dream ended in tatters within minutes of setting out when the coracle capsized on the River Hull, just outside the market town of Beverley. His longing for a new life was not dimmed. Within a few years he set sail for Australia determined to survive by faith as an itinerant preacher. Disillusioned by the intransigent moral laxity of Australia, he made his way to New Zealand and, relying on his unsurpassed manual skills, took up parquetry. Henry's attention was attracted by a young pastry cook who sang cheerfully as she rolled out the dough in the local bakery.

Henry and Esther married and gave birth to Muriel, who inherited Henry's new-found love of parquetry. Muriel used all her measuring and cutting skills to woo a handsome young marquetarian called Jack Cresswell. They married and together became masters of their simple small tools – knives and blades for cutting, and pencil and ruler for making straight lines. But their hands, the hands of angels, were their most sophisticated tools.

I was Jack and Muriel's third and youngest son, born in Wellington on the morning of Monday 13 October 1944. I was not found in a cabinet, but rather cared for and nurtured in one. The same care that my parents gave to their marquetry was lavished on me, although my mother almost poisoned me when, after mixing methanol with dry shellac flakes, she absentmindedly gave me a dose of that instead of kariol.

Marquetry dominated my formative years. Never would we miss the marquetry congress held annually in the Wellington Town Hall. I joined SYMP, the Society of Young Marquetarians and Parquetarians, and it was there, in the evenings that my ears were opened to music. The Marquetry Male Voice Choir sang to us in close harmony, giving vent to the joys and vexations of marquetry. One evening they sang that old Civil War song 'The Vacant Chair'. I was moved and captivated, and then reduced to tears, particularly by these words:

At our fireside, sad and lonely,
Often will the bosom swell
At remembrance of the story
How our noble Willie fell . . .

My eldest brother Max was enchanted by the integrity and logic of structure in parquetry. Roger was fascinated by the function and purpose of marquetry. Musical patterns swirled around in my head as I followed the twirls, whorls, volutes and helixes, and admired the textural colour changes, the rich ornamentation and the patina of age. For a long time I tried to combine the two careers of marquetry and composing music, but the combination became too heavy a burden. After weeks of agonising I was forced to give up marquetry. The symphony was mightier than the cabinet.

Marquetry and Parquetry have always played an important role in my life. They have been both mother and father to me.

My mother used to call her parents Ma and Pa. Their names evoke black iron fireplaces in dark rooms with drawn curtains, fireplace tool sets, coal scuttles, dried flowers, ebony elephants, leather-bound tomes, leather armchairs, rocking chairs, pendulum wall clocks and wooden ball finials. On the wall is a reproduction of William Frederick Yeames' 'And When Did You Last See Your Father?'[1] together with uplifting framed texts on sombre wallpaper such as 'Heirs together of the grace of life', 'A rejoicing heart soon makes a praising tongue', 'The joy of joys is the joy that joys in the joy of others' and from Dorothy Frances Gurney:

The kiss of the sun for pardon,
The song of the birds for mirth,
One is nearer God's heart in a garden,
Than anywhere else on earth.

All this also conjures up the gloomy homes of numerous great-aunts.

An army of great aunts, 1961 – Maggie (grandmother), Lorna (mother's cousin) Chrissie (great aunt), Bert (great uncle), Gerdie (great aunt), Muriel (mother), Doris and Minnie (great aunts). Minnie lived with her sister Jillie and their lodger, Jack Taylor – a thought-provoking arrangement. Whenever we visited them they gave us half a crown each.

My teddy bear, 1947.

My grandfather Henry Proctor Sharp came from a long line of Yorkshire coracle makers. His dream was to build a coracle capable of taking him single-handedly to a new life in America. This dream ended in tatters within minutes of setting out when the coracle capsized on the River Hull, just outside the market town of Beverley. His longing for a new life was not dimmed. Within a few years he set sail for Australia determined to survive by faith as an itinerant preacher. Disillusioned by the intransigent moral laxity of Australia, he made his way to New Zealand and, relying on his unsurpassed manual skills, took up parquetry.

My maternal grandfather, Henry Proctor Sharp was born in Leven near Beverley, in the East Riding of Yorkshire on 28 April 1870. His father, Richard Sharp, was a farm labourer. When Henry was 13 the family emigrated to Australia and settled in Toowoomba where his father established a business as a road contractor. Henry worked in this business until he joined the Salvation Army in 1896 and trained in Melbourne to become a full-time officer. He was sent to work in Auckland in 1897 and remained in New Zealand, taking various posts throughout the country. Preaching and saving souls were important parts of his work. In his diaries of 1902 he records:

> 19 January. A blessed day. Two souls for salvation.
> 21 April. A wonderful meeting . . . with two souls. The glory of God filled the room.

Coracle building and parquetry are red herrings.

Henry Proctor Sharp.

Henry was an upright, upstanding, high-minded, non-drinking, self-denying, non-tobacco-smoking, non-dancing, non-gambling, incorruptible, sober, austere and principled pillar of the church. His spine was stiff, but he was asthmatic. To help alleviate the suffering caused by this condition the doctor suggested he smoke a certain herbal remedy to ease the effects of it and gave him a prescription. After my grandparents died a huge sack of 'Indian Hemp' was found in the basement. This must have done wonders for his spiritual development.

My uncle Richard Sharp told this anecdote about his father:

> Having travelled long distances in the country on a bicycle for the purpose of collecting, he arrived at a household where he was offered some apple juice. As it was particularly hot and the drink very refreshing, Henry drank several glasses in great haste. Approaching home he was seen by the family to be riding in a reckless manner, tunic unbuttoned, waving his cap in the air and in great voice. He was promptly ordered by his wife to take a long bath. The cider was offered to him without appreciating his scruples regarding strong liquor.

The Sharp family: Richard, Herbert and Muriel and their parents, 1930s.

Henry's attention was attracted by a young pastry cook who sang cheerfully as she rolled out the dough in the local bakery.

Eleanor Esther Whitehead[2] was born in Auckland on 11 April 1876. Her grandparents, William and Elizabeth Whitehead, arrived in Auckland from England on 26 September 1859. Her father, also William, was born in 1843. He became a customs official and a committed Methodist. Her mother, Eleanor Hearn Shortt, was born in County Tipperary in 1846 and the family emigrated to New Zealand in 1865. When the Salvation Army started its work in New Zealand William showed interest and introduced his children to it. In 1900 Esther went to the Salvation Army training school in Melbourne.

Henry and Esther were married in 1903. Esther was not a pastry cook and probably had very few cooking skills. Because they were busy with Salvation Army activities they took on Emily Atwood as a domestic helper, nursemaid and cook. She was invited to join them as a teenager because her family was in straitened circumstances after their house burnt down. Emily remained with them until they died and spent the last 10 years of her life in a nursing home in Blenheim. She died at the age of 99.

Eleanor Esther Whitehead, aged 15.

Henry and Esther married and gave birth to Muriel, who inherited Henry's new-found love of parquetry. Muriel used all her measuring and cutting skills to woo a handsome young marquetarian called Jack Cresswell. They married and together became masters of their simple small tools – knives and blades for cutting, and pencil and ruler for making straight lines. But their hands, the hands of angels, were their most sophisticated tools.

Henry and Esther's first child Muriel Minnie was born in Blenheim on 8 May 1905. She married Jack Cecil Cresswell 30 years later. Perhaps they began their marriage with sharp cutting tools, but blunt tools were the norm in the household when I was growing up.

I was Jack and Muriel's third and youngest son, born in Wellington on the morning of Monday 13 October 1944. I was not found in a cabinet, but rather cared for and nurtured in one. The same care that my parents gave to their marquetry was lavished on me, although my mother almost poisoned me when, after mixing methanol with dry shellac flakes, she absentmindedly gave me a dose of that instead of kariol.

I was not poisoned with methanol. I was poisoned with mercury.

Hatmakers, from medieval times to the nineteenth century, used mercury nitrate to cure fur from small animals to make felt for their hats. Inhaling the vapours led to mercury poisoning, which affected the nervous system and could cause such things as shaking, hallucinations, slurred speech and anti-social behaviour. They were often dubbed 'mad hatters'.

Qin Shi Huang, the first emperor of China, is thought to have died from mercury poisoning in his search for the elixir of life. Doses of mercury chloride were responsible for the deaths of George Washington, Louisa May Alcott, Schubert, perhaps Mozart, and many more.

When I was some months old I succumbed to what was known as Pink disease or infantile acrodynia. It was caused by the use of teething powder containing calomel or mercury chloride, which was given to irritable babies. Hands and feet swelled, turned bright pink, itched and prickled. The flesh cracked, the skin peeled back, sweat broke out, blood pressure rose and breathing became difficult. Only about one in every 500 babies given these powders went down with the disease and of those who did, only a few survived. My brother Max told me that there was someone keeping watch over me 24 hours a day. The doctor advised my mother to strap me down when I thrashed around in the cot with irritation, but she would have none of it.

For hundreds of years it was thought that mercury had healing properties. The teething powder business was very profitable and competition was rife. Despite warnings, the various brands claimed that the powders were safe and necessary for the health of growing children. It was only in the 1940s that it was deemed to be toxic and was finally left out of the powders after investigations in the early 1950s.

Some of the lasting complications of Pink disease can be emotional and psychiatric disorders, kidney failure, breakdown of the auto-immune system, co-ordination problems, allergies, skin complaints, respiratory diseases – especially bronchiectasis, and infertility. I have been left with the last two effects and dogged by a permanent cough throughout my life. It is prone to erupt in the middle of a concert and leaves me vulnerable to flu and colds.

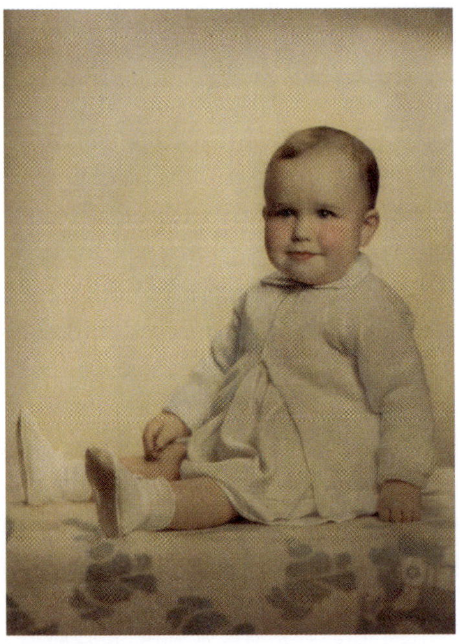

At one year old I was looking slightly less pink.

Marquetry dominated my formative years. Never would we miss the marquetry congress held annually in the Wellington Town Hall. I joined SYMP, the Society of Young Marquetarians and Parquetarians, and it was there, in the evenings that my ears were opened to music. The Marquetry Male Voice Choir sang to us in close harmony, giving vent to the joys and vexations of marquetry. One evening they sang that old Civil War song 'The Vacant Chair'. I was moved and captivated, and then reduced to tears, particularly by these words:

> *At our fireside, sad and lonely,*
> *Often will the bosom swell*
> *At remembrance of the story*
> *How our noble Willie fell . . .*

I have always had a weakness for sentimental songs.

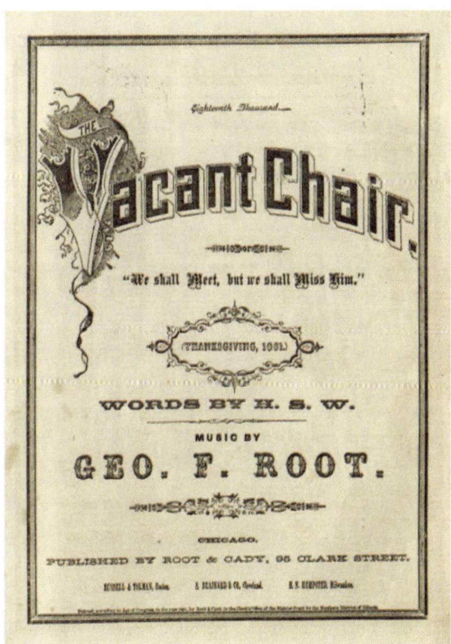

'The Vacant Chair' was one of the most popular songs of the American Civil War. The words were written by Henry Stevenson Washburn in 1861 and set to music by George Frederick Root in 1862. The poem laments the death of John William Grout at the Battle of Ball's Bluff in 1861. George Frederick Root was born in

1820 and named after George Frideric Handel. He was well known for his stirring Civil War songs 'The Battle Cry of Freedom' and 'Tramp! Tramp! Tramp!', and his collaborations with the gospel-hymn writer Fanny Crosby. After brief study in Europe in 1850, Root decided to use the pseudonym G. Friedrich Wurzel to give gravitas to his more genteel compositions.

The Salvation Army used to hold a congress every year in Wellington. Salvationists from all over the country gathered for services, long sermons, affirmations of faith, prayer meetings, children's meetings, street meetings, bible study, sing-songs, tableaux, and concerts with choirs and massed bands. Tears were shed when the male voice choir sang. We were always taken to sit through these long, bottom-numbing events, but it was the marching bands that impressed me most of all.

The Wellington South Salvation band in 1931 or 1932. My father Jack, and my uncles Richard and Herbert Sharp are symmetrically placed – Richard is in the centre of the top row, with Jack and Herbert at the left- and right-hand ends of the middle row.

My eldest brother Max was enchanted by the integrity and logic of structure in parquetry. Roger was fascinated by the function and purpose of marquetry. Musical patterns swirled around in my head as I followed the twirls, whorls, volutes and helixes, and admired the textural colour changes, the rich ornamentation and the patina of age.

Our father was an accountant in the civil service. His enthusiasm for working with reams of abstract symbols was applied to finding ways to fund the building of hydro-electric power stations. His enthusiasm was passed down in different ways to his three sons. Max took the love for abstract symbols to an absurd length and became a logician, and Roger's fascination was in the field of the philosophy of education. My enthusiasm became an obsession with the patterns of musical notation and a more recondite search for a balance between the expression of emotion and intellect through music. Max did the thinking, Roger the ruminating, while I did the dreaming. Our father's search brought him secure employment and a well-ordered life. My search provided a counterbalance of insecurity and disorder.

In Bologna I got to know the philosopher, Roberto Dionigi. When I told him that Max and I were brothers, he said, 'Incredibile, incredibile!' Another time, probably the last time I saw him before he died, he said, 'You are brothers. You have your game. Your brother has his game. I have no game. I am a philosopher.'

My grasp on logic is rather tenuous.

Some years ago Catherine bought a special chair to use for playing the cello – the back legs are a little longer than the front ones. She suggested that we get some castor cups to put under the back legs to make them even longer. I went to the local ironmonger, who delights in not having what one wants, and bought two cups. He looked at me a little oddly. Just as I left the shop I looked at the cups and thought they were a little too subtle, but noticed that one would fit into another to obtain some more height. I returned to the shop and asked for two more. The man looked at me with an expression of contempt as if saying to himself, 'This stupid man doesn't seem to understand that a chair has four legs.'

Parquetry is the art of inlaying wood in geometric patterns, especially for flooring. The most common patterns are herringbone and chevron. Both are laid out in zigzags. In herringbone the wood is cut in rectangles, but for chevron patterns it is cut at an angle to form a parallelogram. Parquet patterns, once set in motion take care of themselves – somewhat like the processes of minimal music.

Marquetry is the art of inlaying contrasting pieces of veneer to create decorative designs or pictures. The pieces can be of bone, ivory, seashell, tortoiseshell, stone, nacre, metal, different types of wood and other exotic materials. Patterns have to be made, knives, saws, drills, cutting mats, pencils, sandpaper and sanding blocks have to be selected, shellac mixtures have to be concocted, glue sorted out, woods chosen and exotic materials found before the pieces can be fitted together like a jigsaw puzzle. In the same way, a piece of music is constructed. Contrasting ideas and motifs are juxtaposed and varied in such a way that when they are assembled they are not perceived as individual pieces.

For a long time I tried to combine the two careers of marquetry and composing music, but the combination became too heavy a burden. After weeks of agonising I was forced to give up marquetry. The symphony was mightier than the cabinet.

I felt the need for further study, this time in Europe, to try to find out if the symphony was indeed mightier than the cabinet. While some chose to sit at the feet of an eminent composer or teacher, I dismissed the idea. I was not looking for a guru and did not want to become the protégé of some great figure – however useful this may have been in promoting my own career. Looking to find my own path and unencumbered by the baggage of the current trendsetters, I enrolled as a PhD student at the University of Aberdeen. Aberdeen was by no stretch of the imagination an obvious place to choose. It is a grey city. The skies are grey, the sea is grey and the granite is grey, but when the sun shines it sparkles, and the wee mannie in the pub buys his friend a drink and says, 'Aye, that's yu're een.' Unlikely though it seemed, I felt this might suit my needs.

The university waived my fees and provided teaching work to give a little income. Catherine found work as a peripatetic cello teacher in schools as far apart as Aberdeen, Fraserburgh and Peterhead. The supervisor for my PhD, Raymond Dodd, was a cellist and composer. He was kind, thoughtful, always ready with helpful suggestions, and let me get on with the work as I pleased. Some years later he told me that I was really teaching him. For younger members of staff, Aberdeen was a stepping stone in their careers. Other students at the time included Lance Olsen, a composition student from Utah, Michael Tumelty, who became an energetic music critic for the *Glasgow Herald* and the basis of a character in a novel by Jilly Cooper, and Kevin Volans, a composer from South Africa.

I was awarded a PhD from the University of Aberdeen in 1974.

In 1973 we were invited to the triennial Musica Nova festival in Glasgow organised by the University of Glasgow and the Royal Scottish National Orchestra. The four featured composers were Luciano Berio, György Ligeti, Peter Maxwell Davies and Martin Dalby. There were discussions, lectures, rehearsals and concerts. It was at this festival that I first met the composer Gillian Whitehead and a strong friendship quickly grew. A list of all those attending the events was available, so we were aware of each other's presence and spent the first day or two circling around looking for a likely candidate. In the end someone introduced us to each other. Gillian

Fellow New Zealand composers Barry Anderson and Gillian Whitehead, Catherine and me, London 1974.

told me that when she first saw my name she thought I was a woman.

Gordon House, a university residence for married students in one of the most expensive streets of Aberdeen was our home. It was a Victorian mansion in splendid grounds built in 1881 for a granite merchant, William Keith.

After the death of her husband in 1934 Ishbel Maria Hamilton-Gordon, Marchioness of Aberdeen and Temair, acquired the house and named it Gordon House. Her husband, John Campbell Hamilton-Gordon, First Marquess of Aberdeen and Temar, and Earl of Aberdeen had been Lord Lieutenant of Ireland and Governor General of Canada. Ishbel was a social reformer with a special interest in women's rights and welfare. She was a spiritualist who communicated with her dead husband through automatic writing, an interest shared by the Canadian Prime Minister, William Lyon MacKenzie King. Before World War II Ishbel set up a spiritualist gathering in Gordon House as a peace mission to try and avert war with Germany. MacKenzie King attended this meeting before going to Berlin to meet Hitler. On his return from Berlin he told the British Prime Minister, Neville Chamberlain that Hitler seemed to be a reasonable man.

As far as we were aware there were no ghosts in the house. The residents came from a number of countries – Venezuela, Nigeria, Sierra Leone, Zimbabwe, Japan, Canada, USA, Greece, England and Scotland. Areas of study included eschatology, jurisprudence, engineering, psychology, soil science, particle physics, medicine, English literature, extreme Christian sects and the behaviour of lice on the heads of oyster catchers.

The housekeeper, Nan, sang in a deep contralto voice as she patrolled and cared for the building and its inhabitants. The winter of 1973–74 was bleak and freezing. It was the time of the three-day working week, the oil crisis, industrial action, coal shortages, power cuts, the troubles in Northern Ireland and a state of emergency. On that dark, dismal and dreich Hogmanay those of us remaining in the house for the festive season huddled together below the staircase of the stately hall to lift the gloom with hot wine and whisky. Nan came to console her brood with wistful Scottish songs. There was not a dry eye in the house when she turned to Ireland and sang 'Danny Boy'. Outside in the snow a merry kilted gentleman cheered us up with his set of miniature bagpipes.

Just down the road lived a lecturer in the psychology department, Norman Wetherick, his wife Mary and their son Donald. They were very kind to us and after I finished my PhD in 1974 offered us the use of a flat at the back of their house.

While Catherine trained as a librarian at Robert Gordon's Institute of Technology, I worked for six months as a hospital theatre porter in Aberdeen Royal Infirmary. My duties involved fetching patients and returning them to the wards after operations, running messages, taking bottles with disgusting-looking contents for analysis, fetching the saw then carrying a suitcase with an amputated limb to the place where it would be taken care of. I was generally at the beck and call of anyone with a white coat. The most onerous task was shaving around the genitals of male patients before they went for the operation. As the most lowly in the hierarchy of theatre porters this job inevitably fell to me. Unlike some of the surgeons, I caused no lasting damage to anyone. Sometimes I was mistaken for a doctor (which I was) and found that if I put on a white coat and carried a pencil I could have free run of the place and peer into all sorts of hospital corners, although such suspect activity was of little interest to me. I had a first-class view in the theatre and could witness with fascination the fine skills and commitment of most of the surgeons.

During quiet periods I hid in the tiny changing closet and read Balzac, but from time to time I was interrupted and castigated by the furious sister, who addressed me as 'Mr Thingy'. One of my jobs was to remove the paper rubbish bags filled with all sorts of refuse and entrails from the theatre, often during operations. Once an overbearing surgeon shouted and swore at me for making an unavoidable rustling noise as I removed the bag. Annoyed by his arrogance I dropped the bag on the floor and walked out. After the operation when he came out of the theatre I wagged my finger at him and told him that 'you can't talk to people like that'. Afterwards he told the other surgeons that he came out and met a large wagging finger. Such behaviour aroused the awe of the other porters and the ire of the sister. After six months in the job I was told that my services were no longer required. The report from the sister said that I showed lack of deference and was of 'below average enthusiasm'. A week or two after I finished at the hospital I went to a concert of chamber music with a friend. A gentleman that I recognised came in and took a seat just in front of us. I whispered to my friend 'I've shaved his balls'. It was impossible for either of us to concentrate and keep still for the rest of the evening.

Catherine was appointed music librarian at Clydebank Library near Glasgow and I was invited to teach at Glasgow University while Stephen Arnold, a contemporary musicologist, took sabbatical leave. And so in 1976 we moved to Glasgow.

The years in Aberdeen were crucial in helping me find my bearings, but I completed no work of any significance there. My fascination with Rotring pens and inks and my interest in graphic work developed. Every Sunday at 4pm the Free Church Gaelic service was broadcast on the radio. I heard for the first time the unique sound of Gaelic psalm singing. This led to the composition of the work with which I began my career in earnest – *Salm*. It was conceived in Aberdeen and written in Glasgow.

Working in Gordon House, 1974.

'Belle, Bonne, Sage' by Baude Cordier.

Intermezzo 1
Graphic Scores

Un nez qui peut voir en vaut deux qui reniflent.
A nose that can see is worth two that sniff.
Eugène Ionesco

A composer writes music down so that someone who has never heard it or seen it before can play it. The notation system invented by Guido d'Arezzo (c.990–c.1050) still forms the basis of modern notation. It has evolved into a system that can be very precise or quite free. For his pains envious monks hounded him out of the Benedictine monastery of Pomposa and he fled to Arezzo.

In the fifteenth and sixteenth centuries, compositions in which the meaning of the music was made visible in the score flourished. Ockeghem and Josquin des Prez, for instance, used blackened notes for laments, or for words like 'dark' and 'night'. Adam Gumpelzhaimer (1559–1625) made scores in the shape of a cross as well as circular ones. Baude Cordier (c.1380–1440) wrote a love song, 'Belle, Bonne, Sage', in the shape of a heart, and in his *Gulliver's Travels* for two violins, Telemann gives the Lilliputians lots of little notes and the Brobdingnagians big slow notes. There are many examples, ancient and modern, of pieces with notation that is intended to make the meaning of the words or ideas visible.

In my student years I was influenced more by the Theatre of the Absurd – people like Eugène Ionesco, Edward Albee and Samuel Beckett – than by John Cage and his coterie. Cage's idea of reducing the control of composers over the music had a certain contradiction since he delighted in being well known and had very definite ideas about the performance of his own music. Ionesco rejected logical plot and character development to convey the futility of existence in a world ruled by chance. But he didn't theorise about his work. He said his plays represent a mood rather than an ideology. Perhaps this approach, with its breakdown of language, makes it closer to music.

Before the days of computer programmes we composed music with pencils, pens, erasers, pencil sharpeners, ink and copious quantities of scrap paper. Once I was satisfied that a piece was finished (as far as this is ever possible) I made the final copy with pen and ink on translucent paper so that vertically ruled sheets could be placed underneath for lining up the notes, and the score could be photocopied using the dieline process.

Copying was a slow process – sometimes I had to rule my own staves, and very occasionally resorted to a woefully inadequate five-pronged nib. This allowed time to reflect on the work and indulge in unrelated doodling on discarded pieces of manuscript paper. The doodles, which became more and more extravagant, sometimes turned into graphic scores, but all this was lost when computers started to make things easier. I am very pleased to have learnt to compose by hand rather than with the aid of the computer.

Graphic scores were in the wind in the 1960s and 70s as guides to improvisation. My attempts were absurd. The scores are completely illogical and irrational and, although nearly all of them have been realised from time to time, my intentions were purely visual. Any resulting music has very little to do with me.

Eye Music (1976), *Nose Music* (1977) and *Ear Music* (c.1980) are large square posters more or less 30 inches by 30 inches. The first two were doodled with no purpose in mind other than, perhaps, therapy. It then seemed logical that they should be followed by *Ear Music.*[1] *Throat Music* came later, but it is a collection of smaller sheets with simple illustrations of gaping mouths and captions such as 'Tonsil and Isolde', 'Goitredämmerung', 'The Jugular of Notre-Dame', 'Dido and Adenoids', 'The Larynx Ascending', 'The Tracheostomy Opera' and so on.

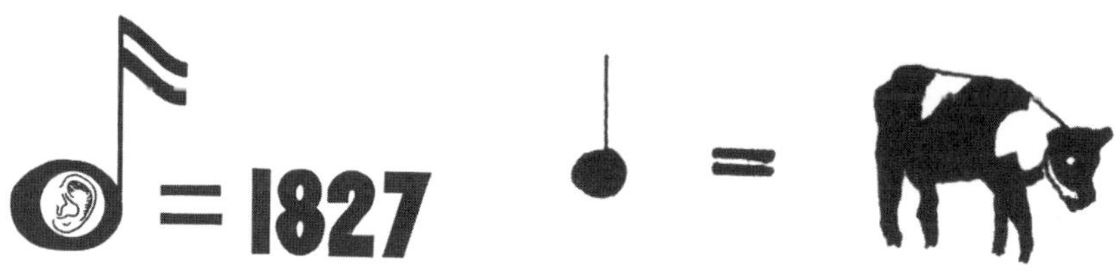

Metronome marks for Eye Music *and* Ear Music.[1]
Nose Music *has no metronome mark.*

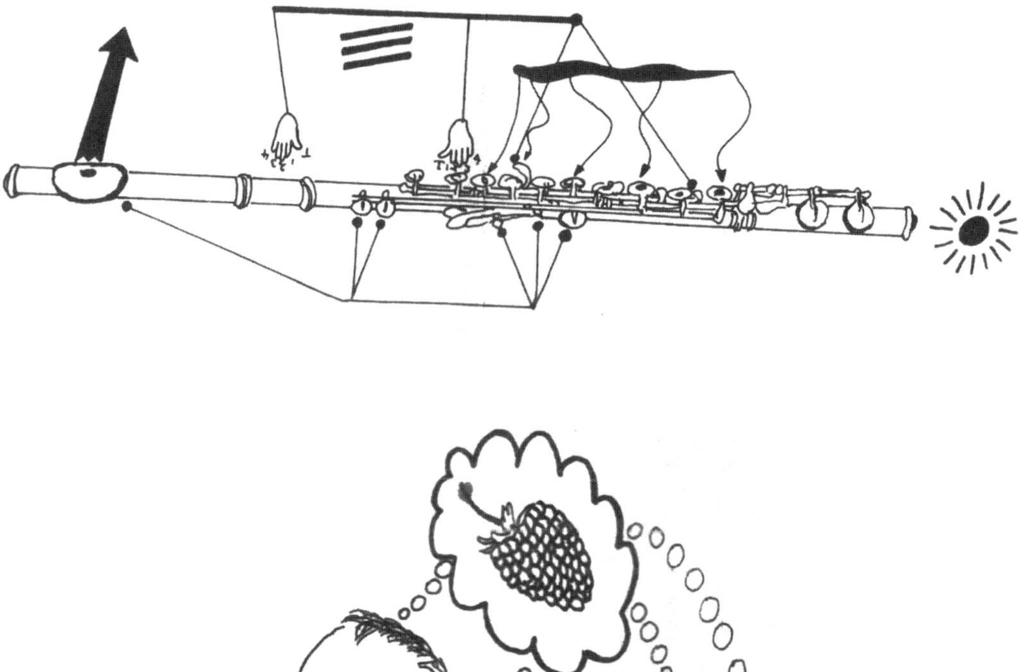

Two details from Eye Music.

Detail from Eye Music.

Some details from Ear Music*:*
'To be seen, but not heard by any number of players'.

Nose Music, dedicated to 'Karlheinz Thingy',[2] contains some written texts such as:

Stretch your nose until it joins your instrument
(don't let your instrument grasp your nose).
Let your nose flow right through the instrument.
Let it fill the whole room in which you are playing.
Let it flow and flow and flow . . .
As long as it flows there will be no error.
Continue as long as it flows
If you continue when the flow has stopped the bucket will
break, this is evil.

Smell the corner of the room which is furthest away from you.
Smell the player next to you
Smell his/her instrument
Smell the vibrations of the universe
Smell May 8, 1968

Everybody smells the same smell.
Take the smell by the nose.
Lead it wherever your ear takes you.
Do not let go of it.
Put it in your instrument – gently
(be careful not to break it)
Whenever it comes out always return it to the instrument.
Breathe.

Three of the 33 pieces from Nose Music.

One of the flats we lived in in Glasgow was at the top of a tenement building with a very resonant stairwell. I recorded some sounds of people climbing the stairs and wrote a piece called *Feet*[1] for 'tape (footsteps) and trombonist with hard-soled shoes' to give to the trombone player Jim Fulkerson.[3] He received it with some bemusement. It is a graphic score interspersed with some lines of music and some Zen stories.

> Two young boys, one from the north and one from the south, crossed paths every day. The one from the north went to learn the trombone.
> One day the boy from the south asked,
> 'Where are you going?'
> 'Wherever my feet will carry me,' replied the boy from the north.
> The boy from the south was silent and went back home pondering over this.
> 'When I meet him tomorrow,' he thought, 'I will ask him the question again.
> And he will give me the same answer – then I will say,
> What if you had no feet – then where would you go?'
> The next day, when the boys met, the boy from the south asked,
> 'Where are you going?'
> 'Wherever the wind will blow me,' was the reply.
> Again the boy from the south was silent and went back home to ponder.
> 'Tomorrow,' he thought, 'I will ask him,
> What if there is no wind?'
> The next day, when the boys met, the boy from the south asked,
> 'Where are you going?'
> The boy from the north replied,
> 'I am going to learn the trombone.'

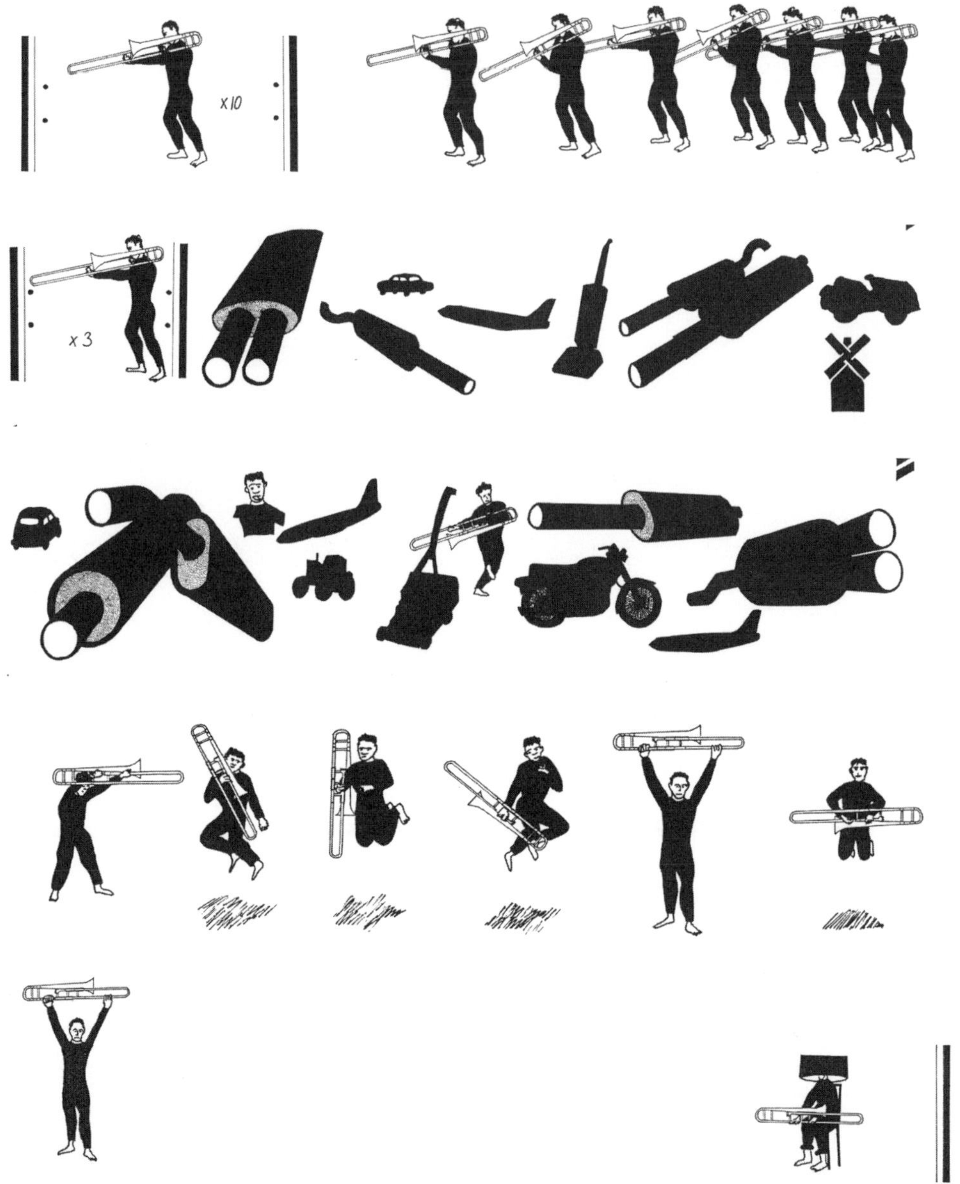

Some details from Feet.

Organic Music, written for Lysis[4] in 1979, is a graphic score for three improvising players. The players chose instruments of wood – symbolised by the tree, skin – the animal and metal – the saucepan. There is no musical notation.

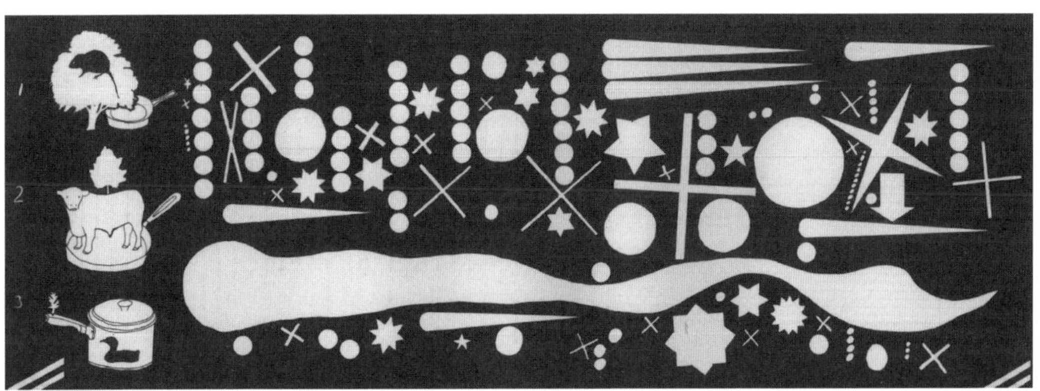

Excerpt from Organic Music.

As a present for Jack Body on his fiftieth birthday in 1994, I made a set of ten drawings,[1] all of which were published in 2012 by Wai-te-ata Music Press.

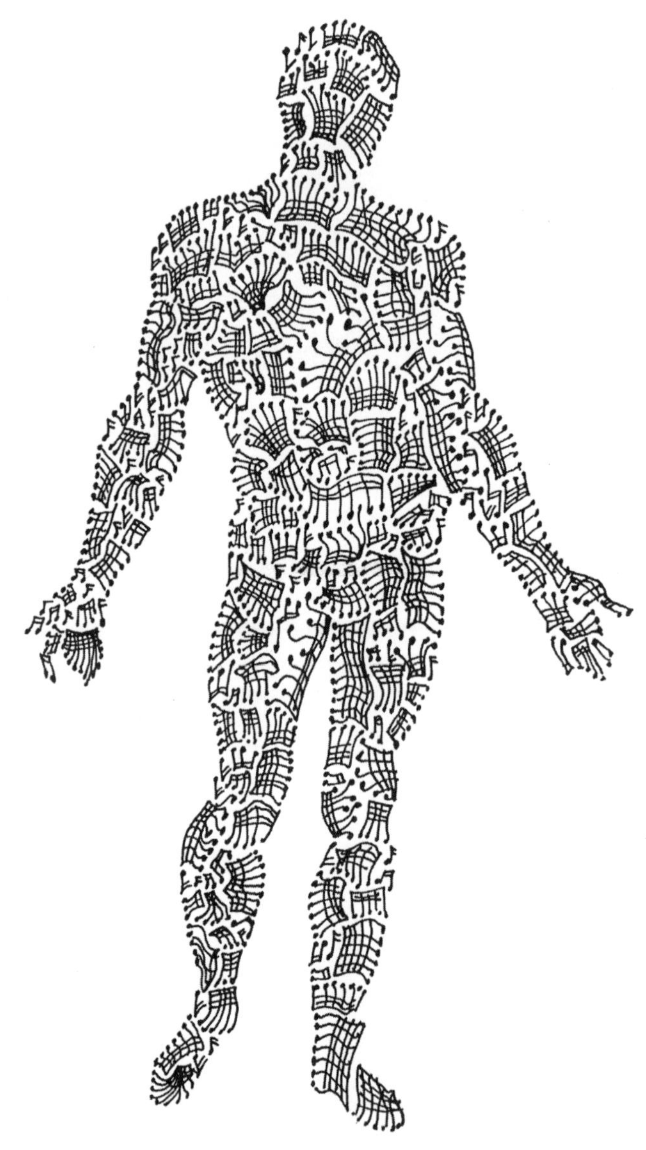

Four drawings from Body Music.

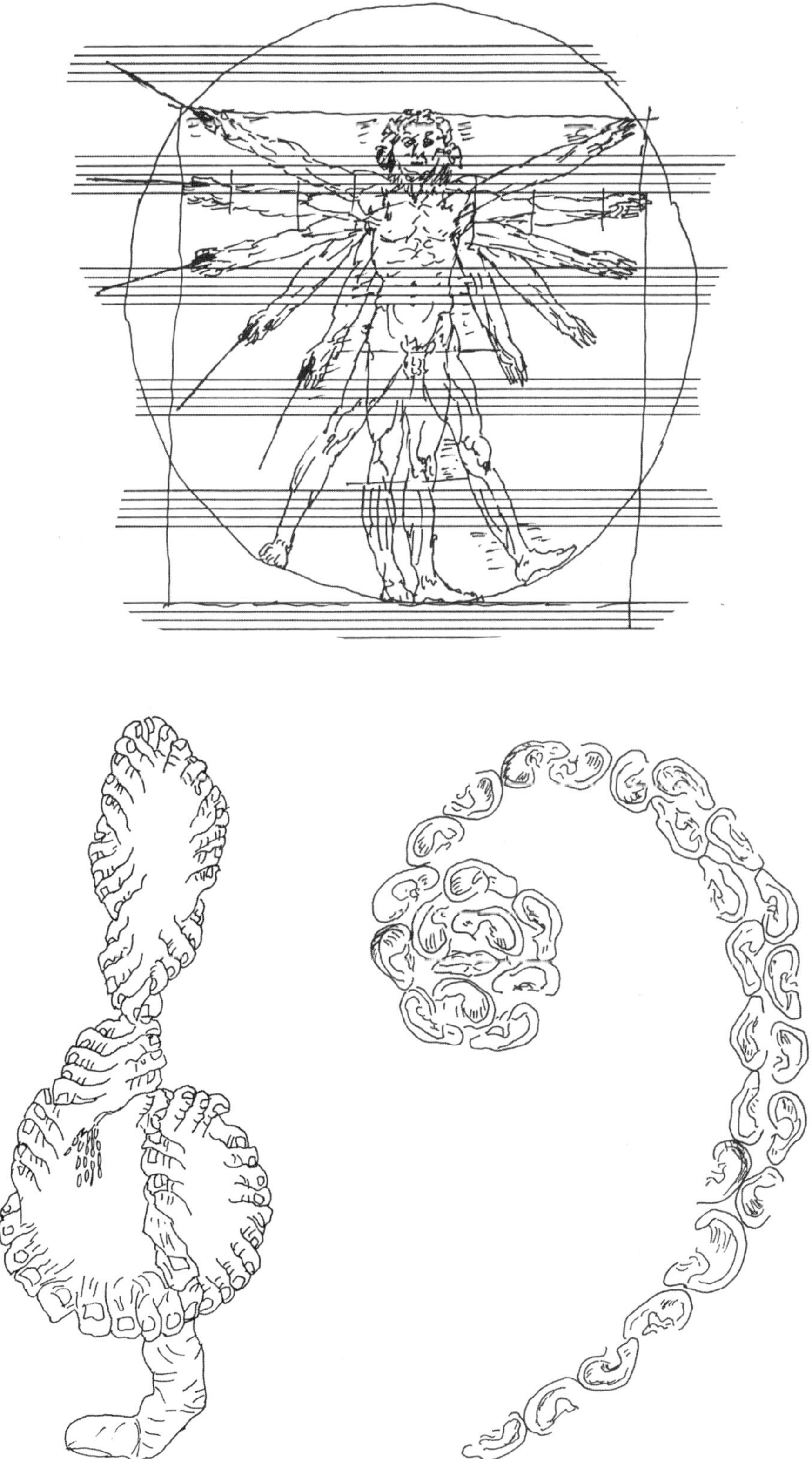

I was in love with my Rotring pens and made little drawings for the title pages of some works. After making one for *The Magical Wooden Head*, a work for strings, brass and percussion, I started fiddling with coloured inks and began a whole series of related drawings.

The magical wooden head, which dwelt on the sacred hill Puketapu had great powers from which no one could escape alive. In Alistair Campbell's[5] telling of the story, the only man to survive its power, before the priest Hakawau defeated the evil spirits from which

Two of the Magical Wooden Head *drawings –*
The head killed them with magic . . .

it derived its power, had done so because he was stone deaf. The music reflects the idea of a being with such enormous powers over the sense of hearing it can cause the death to those who come in search of it.

On the morning of the first rehearsal of *The Magical Wooden Head* by the BBC Scottish Symphony Orchestra in 1984, I woke up deaf in one ear. I had to go to the rehearsal in this condition before the wax could be removed and my hearing restored. Perhaps this was a warning to be careful when dealing with things of the spirit world.

. . . and Hakawau and his servant resting.

The Bach Choir of Wellington, then directed by Roy Tankersley, commissioned a piece for a cappella choir from me in 1980. I set the following Shaker texts, which were written between 1830 and 1850. There is some graphic notation in the last song.

Title page of O Let the Fire Burn, *with a deceptively benign devil.*

1.
Come, let us all unite
To purge out this filthy, fleshy, carnal sense,
And labor for the power of God
To mortify and stain our pride.
We'll raise our glitt'ring swords and fight
And war the flesh with all our might,
All carnal ties we now will break
And in the power of God we'll shake.

2.
Now I will bow low,
Now I will bow low,
Now I will bow low,
Yea I will,
That heavenly blessings
My soul may fill.

3.
Shake! Shake! Shake in the valley.
Shake down low.
Shake! Shake! Shake in the valley.
Shake off pride!
Shake off the flesh.

Come down shaker-like,
Come down holy,
Come down shaker-like,
Let's all go to glory.

4.
Vi ve vo, vi ve vum
Vi ve vum, vi ve vo,
Vi ve vo, vi ve vum.
Vi ve vum, vi ve vo,

Oh ho ho ho!
Haw ew oh hoo,
Aw ew aw hoo hoo.
Aw ew aw, ew ew oh,
Aw ew aw ew oh oh
Ho oh a oo

5.
O let the fire burn,
Hotter the better,
O let the fire burn,
Burn up all that's evil.

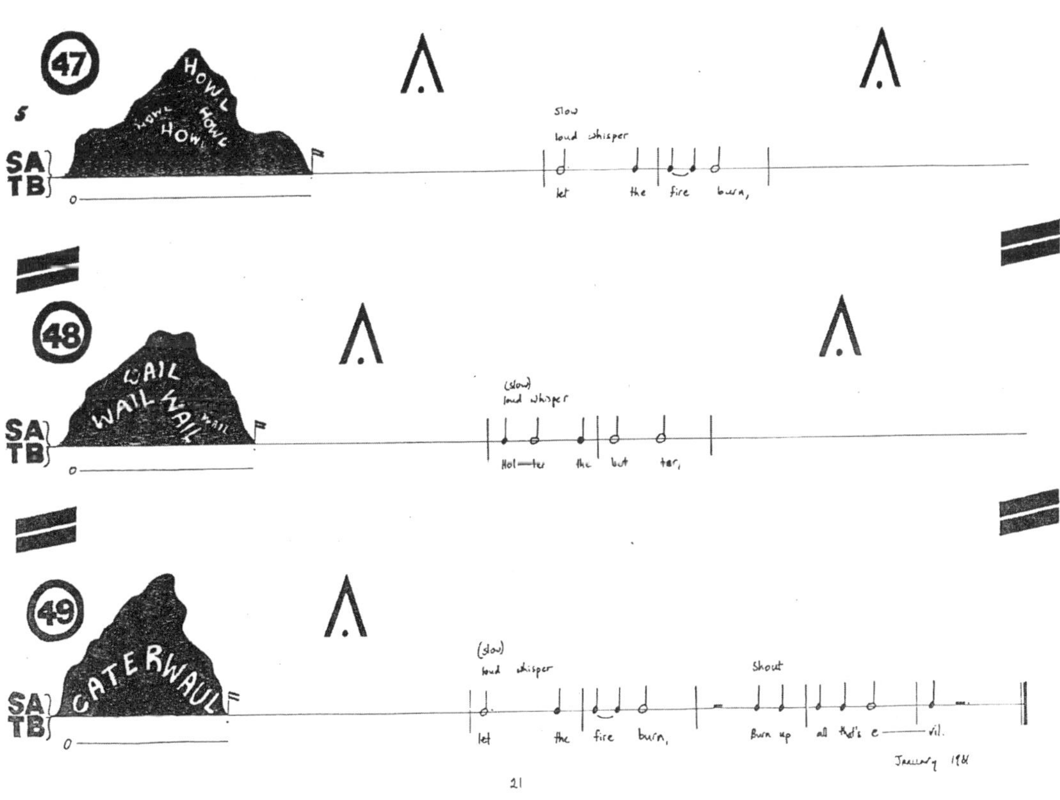

Detail from the final song.

My only brush with film music was making electronic soundtracks for three animated films by the Glasgow animated film maker, Lesley Keen – *Taking a line for a walk* (based on the work of Paul Klee), *Orpheus and Eurydice* and *Invocation*. After a lot of discussion and experiment Lesley gave me the storyboard, I made the soundtrack in the studio at Glasgow University and she adjusted the final animation to fit the music.

A still from Lesley Keen's animation, Taking a line for a walk.
Lesley Keen

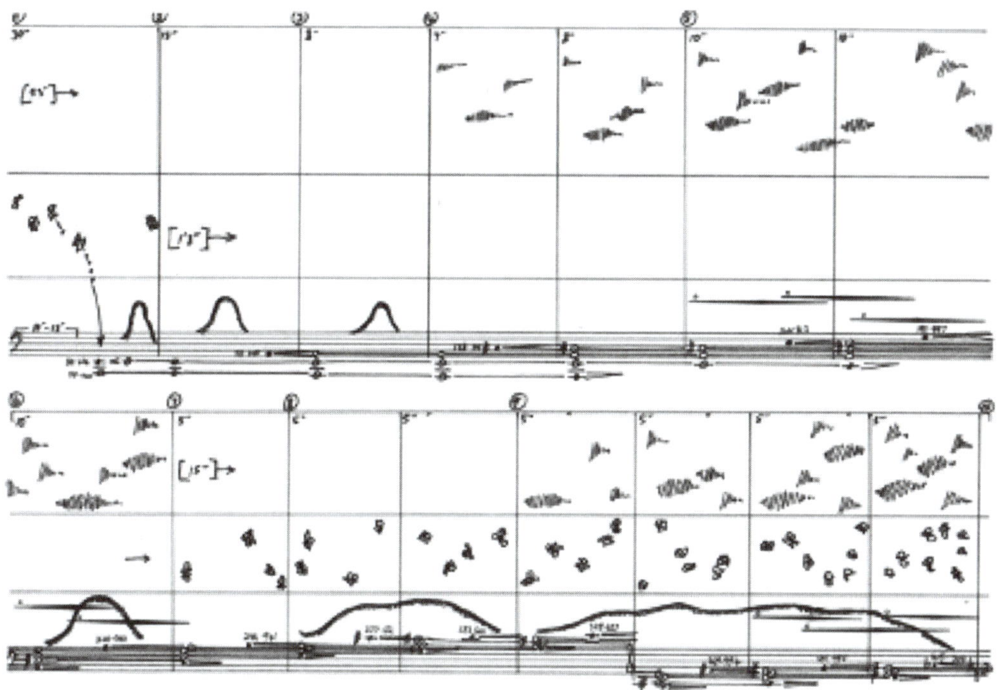

Working drawings for Taking a line for a walk.

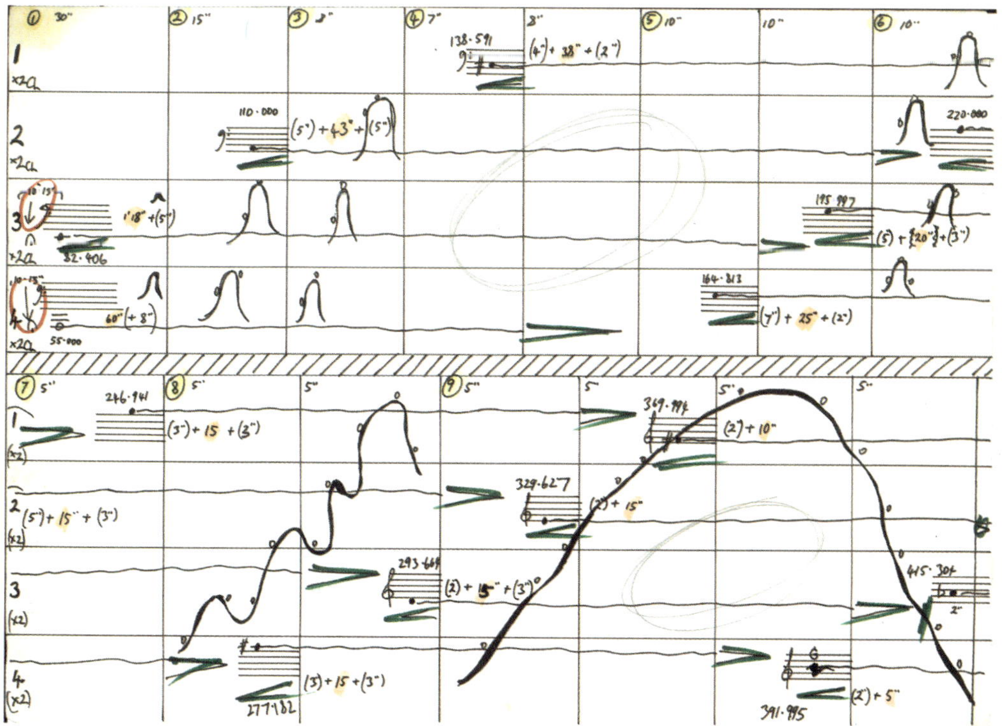

A page from the score of Taking a line for a walk.

Threnody for Mrs S – who was drowned at her Baptism was written in 1971 or 1972 and is scored for piccolo, flute, cor anglais, clarinet, bass clarinet, bassoon, contrabassoon, horn, trumpet, trombone, xylophone, harp and speaker. It is not a graphic score, but there are a few traces lurking.

The speaker relates the story.

June the third – A fifty-seven-year-old clergyman was sentenced to one hundred days imprisonment today for drowning Mrs S____ when he baptized her in a nearby river on April the twenty-ninth.

The clergyman said that in the past twenty-seven years he had baptized many people but Mrs S____ was the first who had drowned.

The court was told that she was dipped in the water several times as the clergyman prayed.
. . . . and they went down both into the water.

Dip, duck, dunk, immerse, souse, plunge, submerge, Baptize, drown.

I baptize thee in the name of the Father, and of the Son, and of the Holy Ghost. Amen.

Shall we gather at the river,
Where bright angel feet have trod,
With its crystal tide forever
Flowing by the throne of God.

Lux aeterna luceat eis, Domine: Cum Sanctis tuis in aeternum: quia pius es.

From the french horn part of Threnody for Mrs S
– who was drowned at her Baptism.

Chapter 4
Tuesday 13 October 1944

Some men there are love not a gaping pig;
Some, that are mad if they behold a cat;
And others, when the bag-pipe sings i' th' nose,
Cannot contain their urine.
Shakespeare, The Merchant of Venice*, Act 4 Scene 1*

The date and place of my birth is not certain, but it is reckoned to be Tuesday 13 October 1944 at about 30 degrees south of the equator near the 180th meridian – very close in fact to the International Date Line – at an altitude of about 10,000 feet. We were in a flying boat, travelling from Suva to Auckland in the wake of unfounded rumours of an imminent Japanese invasion. I was born to the drone of a Boeing 314 Clipper flying boat. Prior to that I knew only the shrouded boom of my mother's deep-bosomed contralto voice as her melancholy ballads reached me in the womb.

My father Jack Cresswell was an itinerant comparative philologist specialising in Vedic Sanskrit. He had a passion for 16mm home movies and was an admirer of the writing of Oswald Spengler.[1] Jack had been sent to Fiji to assist with the deciphering of Japanese coded messages. My mother Muriel Sharp had been the first woman student to graduate in classics at the University of Auckland. She took a particular interest in the ancient Greek musical scholar Aristoxenus. Paul Henry Lang, in his incisive survey *Music in Western Civilization*, says that 'as a man, Aristoxenus was not attractive and his fellow citizens considered him a quarrelsome, envious and malignant individual'. I think it is these qualities that endeared him to my mother.

The heady atmosphere into which I was born made it inevitable that I should be a precocious child. My first words were spoken at the age of 11 months. Looking out of the window one day I said, 'There is so much room to die.' Some would have it that what I really said was, 'There is so much room today,' but even at that early age, both the concept of death and an understanding of the relationship between time and space had entered my enormous mind.

After brilliant progress through school and university, I obtained a Fulbright Scholarship to study quantum chromodynamics and the interactive behaviour of quarks at the Massachusetts Institute of Technology. In 1967 I was a trialist for the All Black rugby tour of the United Kingdom playing at first five-eighth.

Parallel to these things I kept an interest in music. My musical career began at the age of four, when I gave a recital on a Wheatstone concertina to a packed audience in the Karori Returned Services Association (RSA) Hall. Thereafter I was seduced by the call to compose.

The date and place of my birth is not certain, but it is reckoned to be Tuesday 13 October 1944 at about 30 degrees south of the equator near the 180th meridian – very close in fact to the International Date Line at an altitude of about 10,000 feet. We were in a flying boat, travelling from Suva to Auckland in the wake of unfounded rumours of an imminent Japanese invasion. I was born to the drone of a Boeing 314 Clipper flying boat.

Drones suggest bagpipes.

MacCrimmon is a most venerable name in Scottish piping. Much of the early pìobaireachd (pibroch) or classical pipe music has been attributed to members of this family. According to one story the name comes from Cremona and the family is descended from a priest called Giuseppe Bruno. Giuseppe's brother, Giordano, was a freethinking philosopher who was tried for heresy in 1593 and after a seven-year trial burned at the stake in Rome. James Joyce admired and was influenced by the theories of Giordano. Giuseppe's son Petrus was a harp player and shared some of his uncle's beliefs. While Giordano's trial was in progress Petrus decamped to Ireland, where he changed his name to Patrick and married into an Irish piping family before being lured to the Isle of Skye by the MacLeods. The story tells that Patrick had a son, Donald Mór MacCrimmon, who was a renowned player and composer of pìobaireachd. Donald had an adventurous life. After setting fire to a village in Kintail in revenge for the murder of his brother by the MacKenzies, he fled to the far north of Scotland, broke into a house and hid in a wardrobe. Later that night the plangent sound of the chanter playing Donald's own dirge, *Too Long in this Condition,* percolated through the wardrobe door and fell on sympathetic ears. He was saved and pardoned.

One day a bagpiper came to see me. He was a friend of a friend of a friend and was interested in exploring new techniques for the bagpipe. After showing me a few tricks he asked if I would write something for him. The challenge was irresistible. I asked for the drones to be tuned to the interval of a major second, included most of the tricks he had showed me and called the piece *Not Long in this Condition*. When I gave it to him he said it was 'more or less playable', but I didn't hear from him again. All that remained of his visit was a small round tin emitting a rather curious smell. It contained the thick brown syrup used to keep the bag airtight and to absorb moisture from the breath. The recipe for bagpipe seasoning might contain such ingredients as lanolin, honey, molasses, glycerine, lye, oil soap, raw cane sugar, bone glue and 100 per cent proof whisky.

Another venture into writing for the pipes was a commission for the opening of the 1999 European Foundation for Management Development Annual Conference at the University of Edinburgh Management School, organised by a friend, Professor James Fleck.

The piece was called *Gathering Music.* In his *Compleat Theory of the Scots Highland Bagpipe,* published in 1803, Joseph MacDonald writes:

> Gatherings . . . are the most animated of pipe compositions, as they were originally intended to assemble the Highlanders under their respective chiefs upon any emergency, and indeed, they answered the purpose, being very well adapted for it.
>
> Every chief had a Gathering for his name, which are so full of life, that no music can be more animating.

and . . .

> Bagpipe music, well executed, has a much more martial effect than horns or trumpets. Their music and tone seem more pacifick being neither so stimulating nor furious as the warlike compositions on the bagpipe, the prodigious loudness of which, in a field, especially when three or four are joined & the music well executed, has a glorious effect in advancing on the enemy.

I met the young piper who was to play the piece and his rather dour teacher. As it turned out everything I had written was playable – no experimental techniques were involved – but when the teacher looked at it, he said, 'Och noo, ye cannae dee that.' Later I took this music and turned it into part of a little orchestral piece – *The Rev Norman McLeod's Dance.*

Lithuanian composer Anatolijus Šenderovas with miniature bagpipes at his home in Nemenčinė, July 2005.

In November 2004 Anatolijus presented a concert of chamber music by both of us in the Vilnius Town Hall.

Prior to that I knew only the shrouded boom of my mother's deep-bosomed contralto voice as her melancholy ballads reached me in the womb.

Hymns and patriotic songs – for example, 'Sword and buckler by my side, Rest on the shore of battle-tide' from *Merrie England* by Edward German – made up my mother's repertoire as she went about her daily chores. I cringed one holiday when she burst into 'Praise, my soul the King of heaven' in front of an audience of glow worms and tourists in the Waitomo Caves.

From the womb the sounds of brass bands playing tone poems and rousing marches would have reached me, along with the drone of long sermons.

My father Jack Cresswell was an itinerant comparative philologist specialising in Vedic Sanskrit. He had a passion for 16mm home movies and was an admirer of the writing of Oswald Spengler.

Jack was the youngest of four siblings – the others were Ivy, and twins Frank and Ray. Frank was very keen on 16mm home movies. He documented family gatherings and had a repertoire of silent movies including the Keystone Cops, Fatty Arbuckle, Charlie Chaplin, Laurel and Hardy and so on. I remember particularly the footprints in the sand of the 1927 *Robinson Crusoe,* which Marmaduke Arundel Wetherell directed, produced and starred in. Wetherell was also responsible for the 'surgeon's photograph' hoax of the Loch Ness Monster.[2] Quite often we sat waiting patiently as a broken film was repaired or the projector overheated.

My father had no interest in the writings of Oswald Spengler.

Jack had been sent to Fiji to assist with the deciphering of Japanese coded messages. My mother Muriel Sharp had been the first woman student to graduate in classics at the University of Auckland.

Muriel did not graduate in classics or anything else from the University of Auckland, but my father's sister Ivy graduated with an MA in Latin and French from Canterbury College of the University of New Zealand in 1929. In the 1940s she was a Salvation Army missionary school teacher in Kenya. While there, one of her escapades was to climb Mount Kilimanjaro without an oxygen mask.

Ivy in Kenya.

She took a particular interest in the ancient Greek musical scholar Aristoxenus. Paul Henry Lang, in his incisive survey Music in Western Civilization, *says that 'as a man, Aristoxenus was not attractive and his fellow citizens considered him a quarrelsome, envious and malignant individual.' I think it is these qualities that endeared him to my mother.*

I have had a copy of Paul Henry Lang's magnificent tome *Music in Western Civilization* since student days and consulted it countless times on all manner of things. It is said that the philosopher and musical theorist Aristoxenus was bitterly disappointed when Aristotle did not choose him as his successor. This seems to have been the cause of great rancour, but very little else is known about his life.

The heady atmosphere into which I was born made it inevitable that I should be a precocious child. My first words were spoken at the age of 11 months. Looking out of the window one day I said, 'There is so much room to die.' Some would have it that what I really said was, 'There is so much room today,' but even at that early age, both the concept of death and an understanding of the relationship between time and space had entered my enormous mind.

The joy shown by my parents when I read, 'Too much spoils the flavour' on the Marmite bottle surprised me. I was three or four, and knew I could read. At 11 months I had no profound thoughts.

After brilliant progress through school and university, I obtained a Fulbright Scholarship to study quantum chromodynamics and the interactive behaviour of quarks at the Massachusetts Institute of Technology.

In the summer of 1982 I obtained a Scottish Arts Council grant to take the computer music course at the Massachusetts Institute of Technology. Two Scots, Brian Anderson, a promising young composer who was tragically killed in an accident on Ben Nevis soon after, and Peter Nelson, a composer and distinguished academic, also took the course. I wanted to test my relationship with technology once again.

Previously, for the academic year of 1974–75, I had received a Dutch Government Bursary to study at the Institute of Sonology in Utrecht. Through the university we found a room in a former nursing home in the leafy, well-to-do village of Bilthoven. On one side of the main highway the streets are named after composers, but on our side they are named after painters. There is Pieter Breughellaan, Van Dijklaan, Jan van Eijcklaan, Frans Halslaan, Hans Memlinglaan, Rubenslaan, Vermeerlaan, Rogier van der Weydenlaan and Rembrandtlaan, where we lived. The house was owned and cared for by Zuster Balk, a small elderly lady always dressed in black. The cellar was jam-packed with tinned food and long-life milk. What secrets might it have kept, and what must Zuster Balk have witnessed and endured during World War II?

At the Institute of Sonology there were absorbing lectures. As well as composers there were researchers working on programming, psychomusicology, voice and instrument synthesis, live electronic performance and all things digital. Fascinating though this was I was not drawn to following a technological path since this would mean relying on assistance and computer programmes designed by others. I am not technologically minded and prefer working with the sounds of traditional instruments in the hands of musicians.

At the Easter break there was a special offer for students to fly to Athens. It involved getting a train to Paris and a flight to Athens via Copenhagen – circuitous, but cheap. We were invited to stay with friends in Athens.

On 25 March 1975, for the first time since the fall of the repressive right-wing junta or Régime of the Colonels,[3] there was a rally in Athens marking Independence Day – the struggle for Greek independence from the Ottoman Empire began on 25 March 1821. The atmosphere was festive with blue-and-white flags everywhere, and music and dancing in the streets.

The Greek composer Iannis Xenakis suffered horrific injuries fighting against the brutal British occupation, which turned against the partisans that they had supported during the war. He was forced into exile in Paris in 1947. In March 1975 he returned to Greece and gave a lecture to a wide audience, including us. The lecture was not confined to musical matters, but he told us that when he went into exile his only hope was in his work, that he regarded himself as a citizen of the world and that his life was dedicated to music.

Our return to Bilthoven was tortuous. The flight to Paris arrived late and we missed the train connection to Utrecht. Instead we arrived in Rotterdam in a snow storm late at night with no money for a hotel. We found a bar open until 2am then, after walking around, ended up huddled on the stairs to the basement of a tower block where the dossers slept, keeping us awake with a chorus of snores and sputters. We almost slept through Utrecht station on our return.

Summer in Boston in 1982 was very hot, with temperatures over 100 Fahrenheit. To warm the studio at the Massachusetts Institute of Technology, rather than turn off the fierce air-conditioning, we had to fling the windows open. It struck me as odd that in this hothouse of technological innovation this was the method that had to be used. The American students could not comprehend our amusement at the idea of opening windows to warm up.

As in Utrecht there were stimulating lectures and discussions. The course involved composing a piece using computer-generated sounds to which I added a piano. The file I created was described by the keen young men assisting as 'humungous', but I was not at all happy with the result. Once again I came to the conclusion that this was not my métier.

At the end of the course Catherine joined me in Boston and we took some time to visit the Shaker village of Canterbury in New Hampshire – perhaps the best preserved and least touristic of these villages. There we met Eldress Gertrude, one of the very last Shakers.

She had been well known for her storytelling, which shed light on the ways of the Shakers, but she was old and frail, and it would have been insensitive to pry.

In 1967 I was a trialist for the All Black rugby tour of the United Kingdom playing at first five-eighth.

In 1957 at Karori West Primary School a keen parent decided to start up a Saturday morning soccer team, which I joined. Only rugby was played at the school. This team was known as Tech Old Boys – we had our practice in the gym of the Wellington Technical College. I always used to dodge to the back of the line when it came to practising unpleasant things like taking the ball on our heads or chests. We were taken to the games in the back of an old covered pickup truck. On the way home we used to stop and wait around for about an hour while the men went off on some mysterious business. In my innocence I didn't realise at first that they were going to the pub – this was unheard of in my teetotal family. At our first game I was positioned somewhere out of harm's way at the back. The ball was kicked into the penalty area near me. My instinctive reaction was to bend down and pick it up with my hands. Eyes rolled. The resulting penalty was the first of many goals scored against our team during the course of the season.

After 1957 I didn't play football again until one Saturday afternoon in 2012 on the Meadows in Edinburgh. I was inveigled into playing a game with various literary types including Ron Butlin and Ian Rankin. It turned into a filthy wet afternoon and we lolloped around in the mud. At one point during the match, when I was running for the ball, a huge man about twice my size just ran up and bumped me out of the way – so much for a friendly bit of fun. The competitive spirit soon took over in no uncertain terms. I could see nothing through my wet glasses, so took them off and played the rest of the game with a Monet-like view of the pitch. Catherine appeared during the game. While she was watching on the sideline a passer-by came up to her and said 'You have to admire them. Look at that one!' as he pointed to me. This was the end of my football career. My short careers in hockey, fencing and cricket followed similarly undistinguished paths, although my liking for cricket remains.

When I am travelling and if work is involved, I take my lovely old wind-up stopwatch with me. Once at Edinburgh airport the security man spotted it in my bag, looked at it and asked, 'Do you do a bit of refereeing?'

I took my stopwatch to the 2019 Michael Hill International Violin Conpetition in Queenstown. I thought I might time the contestants playing Chatoyance, the five-minute test piece I had written for the competition.
Clarissa Dunn, courtesy of RNZ Concert

My chess playing is just a little better. For quite a long time I played postal games with Ted Middleton in Dunedin. These games could last years because there would be weeks between moves, but they were a good way of keeping in touch.

Now I play slow chess by email with Dutch violinist Kees Hilhorst. Kees spent some time living in New Zealand earlier this century. We use a very particular notation for these games, which started normally but gradually the pieces acquired names like Achilles, Ivanka, Neve Gayford or Vladimir. Since then they have become more and more absurd. There is plenty of scope for confusion. Here, for instance are the first six moves of a game. Kees is playing white.

1. Karl-Heinz moves two steps ahead of King Iannis, Sancho moves two steps ahead of King Alfonso the Fat.
2. Honorius o Terciero jumps in the field, two fields diagonally from King Iannis, Götz von Berlichingen leaps over minions into action to wag his long fingers at Karl-Heinz.
3. Donald Tusk tweets twice from Iannis' Orient to blame Sancho's game: an aggressive reply, Sancho removes the annoying Donald Tusk.

4. Lola Montez leaves King Iannis and dances to a field ahead of Honorius o Terciero. The mysterious flunky of Queen Loana takes a little step forward.
5. Lola Montez aborts Nicoletta Bodoni the little girl next to King Alfonso the Fat, King Alfonso the Fat obliterates Lola Montez.
6. Dr Schnee comes two electrifying steps closer to Queen Loana. The mysterious flunky of Queen Loana takes one small step for man.

Parallel to these things I kept an interest in music. My musical career began at the age of four, when I gave a recital on a Wheatstone concertina to a packed audience in the Karori RSA Hall.

Sir Charles Wheatstone was an ingenious inventor. Among other things he invented a stereoscope, a cryptograph, the Wheatstone Bridge to measure electrical resistance, and in 1830 the concertina. The concertina became very popular and was used a lot by the Salvation Army. The early bands were often made up of concertinas rather than brass instruments. Aunt Ivy gave me a Wheatstone concertina when I was still at primary school. At that time, for just one year I joined the St John Ambulance cadets. We met in the Karori RSA Hall and learnt about fractures and how to make slings for a broken arm. I did not play my concertina there, nor did I play it to an audience anywhere else.

My Wheatstone concertina.

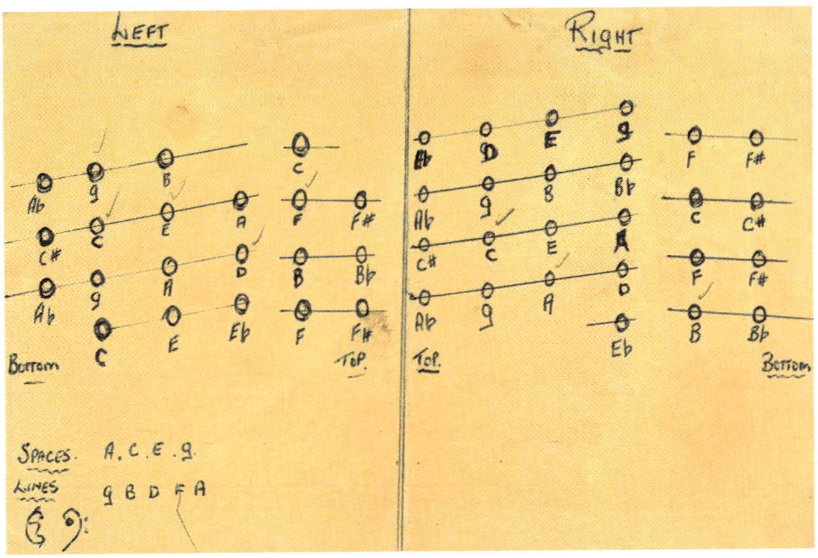

The button pattern for the Wheatstone concertina.

Thereafter I was seduced by the call to compose.

Composers are both philosophers and storytellers. Philosophers articulate and clarify difficult concepts, and interpret the thoughts and feelings peculiar to their own time. Storytellers recount series of connected events, set up and explore and resolve ideas, or depict moods and atmospheres. Composers are not anaesthetists who put people to sleep while something is being done to them for their own good.

Beginning work on a new composition is always difficult. First I look at the things I know – who has commissioned the work, what the forces are – instruments or singers – and the duration, then I shilly-shally. I look for any excuse not to work. I doodle, drink coffee, clear the desk, make lists, tidy up, stand on one leg, do the crossword, have a snooze, play with the cat, practise left-hand writing, take a walk, go to the pub or just watch paint drying. Eventually I pull myself together and make charts, draw sketches, make timetables, scribble random jottings, plot diagrams and graphs, then tear them all up and make new ones to tear up. I wrestle and fiddle. I fiddle with notes, chords, scales, rhythms, numbers, shapes, pencils, pens, markers, rulers, calculator, stopwatch, piano and computer. I fiddle until a scheme reveals itself and tells me what to do. Every piece must find its own scheme. Once I have what seems to be a clear-cut plan I can begin, but the plan evolves as the composition progresses and sometimes takes unexpected turnings. I work from the middle until it becomes clear how the music should begin and how it should end. No scheme, however well thought out, can be followed strictly. In the end corrections must be made by ear.

The orchestra has one of the greatest concentrations of highly skilled people working together on one interdependent activity. Writing for it still provides the most sophisticated and challenging means of musical expression. It makes for a confrontation between the composer and the manuscript paper. The sounds, the subtle mingling of different instruments and all the complexities have to be imagined before they can be written down. These things cannot be found with the use of a computer programme, and since the music can only be heard properly once the orchestra is assembled, it pushes all of the composer's resources to their limits.

In 2002 I was awarded the inaugural Elgar Bursary. The bursary was set up with the revenue from Anthony Payne's realisation of Elgar's third symphony in 1997. The press release from the Royal Philharmonic Society announcing the award said, 'The decision to award the first bursary to Lyell Cresswell was unanimous: a reflection of our admiration for his independent, individual musical voice.'

English composer, Anthony Payne (1936–2021). Jane Manning

This led to a commission for the BBC Symphony Orchestra. I wrote a one-movement piece lasting just over 20 minutes – *Ara Kōpikopiko*, meaning labyrinth. It is made up of a number of ideas that weave in and out of one another, sometimes overlapping and sometimes reaching a dead end. The outcome is something like a piece of marquetry comprising small pieces of shell, ivory, ebony, mahogany, mother of pearl, jade or agate fitted together to form an integrated but mottled picture.

The piece is put together in 20 merging sections making the following pattern: A B C D C A B C D A C A D A C B A D B D.

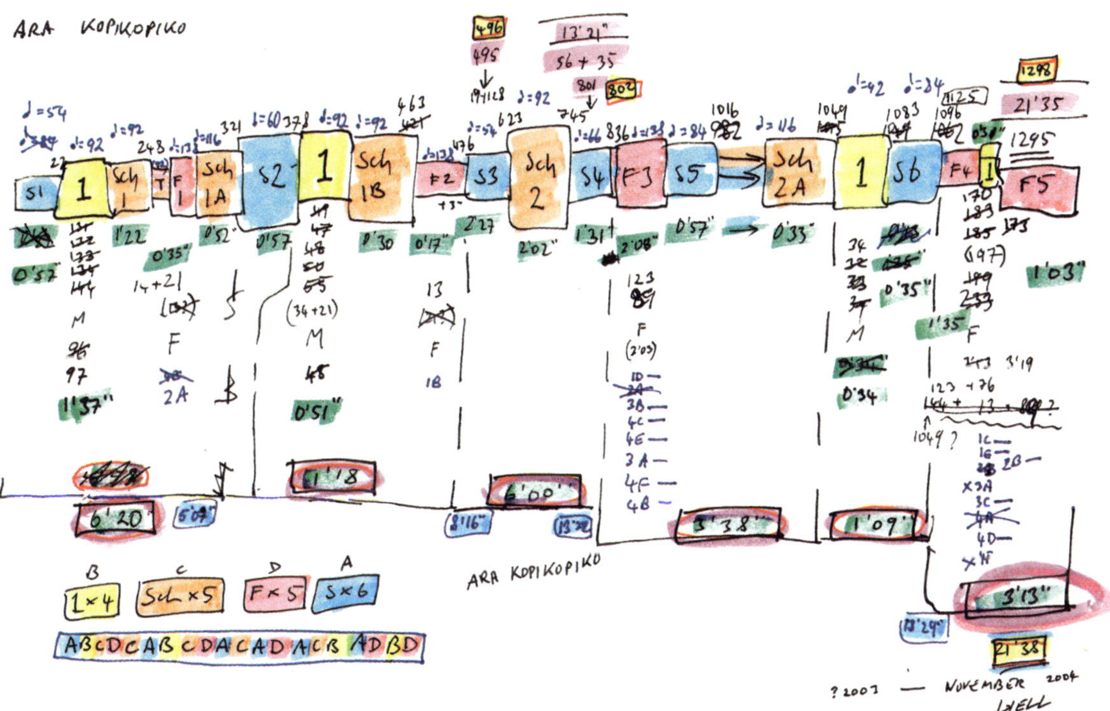

Work plan and timings for Ara Kōpikopiko.

Two orchestral works with a soloist, *Kāea* and *Alas! How Swift*, were written nine years apart. Both are for a solo brass instrument and chamber orchestra. *Kāea*, a concerto for trombone, was commissioned by the Scottish Chamber Orchestra for the Swedish trombone player, Christian Lindberg in 1997. The pūkāea, or kāea, is a long wooden trumpet used by Māori to raise the alarm in times of danger.

Kāea – *harmonic scheming.*

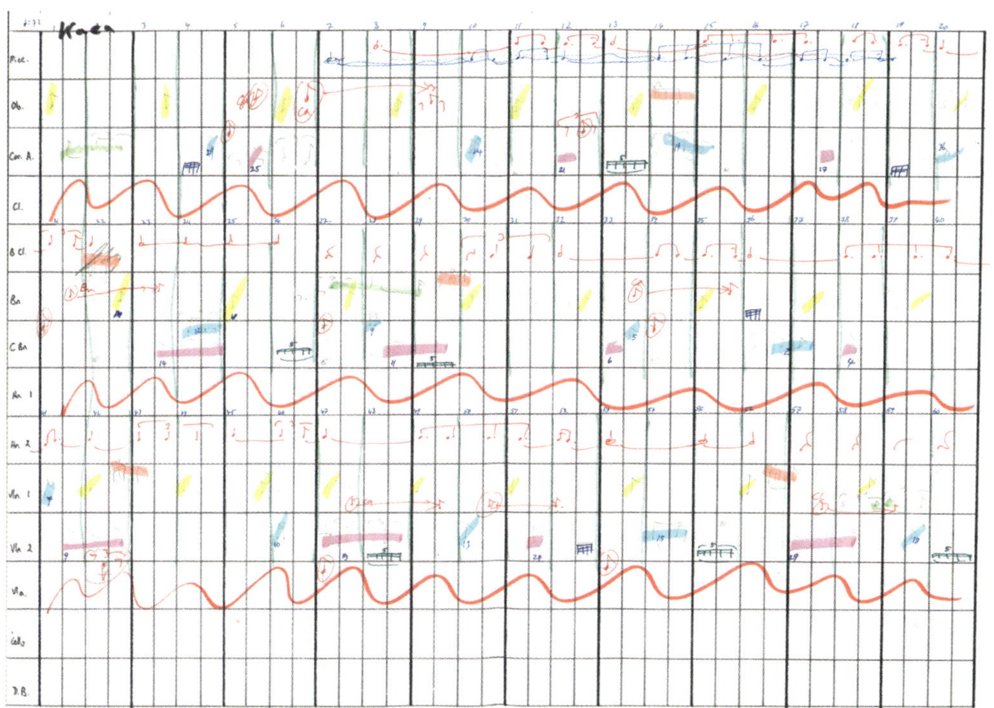

Kāea – *plotting motifs and recurring fragments.*

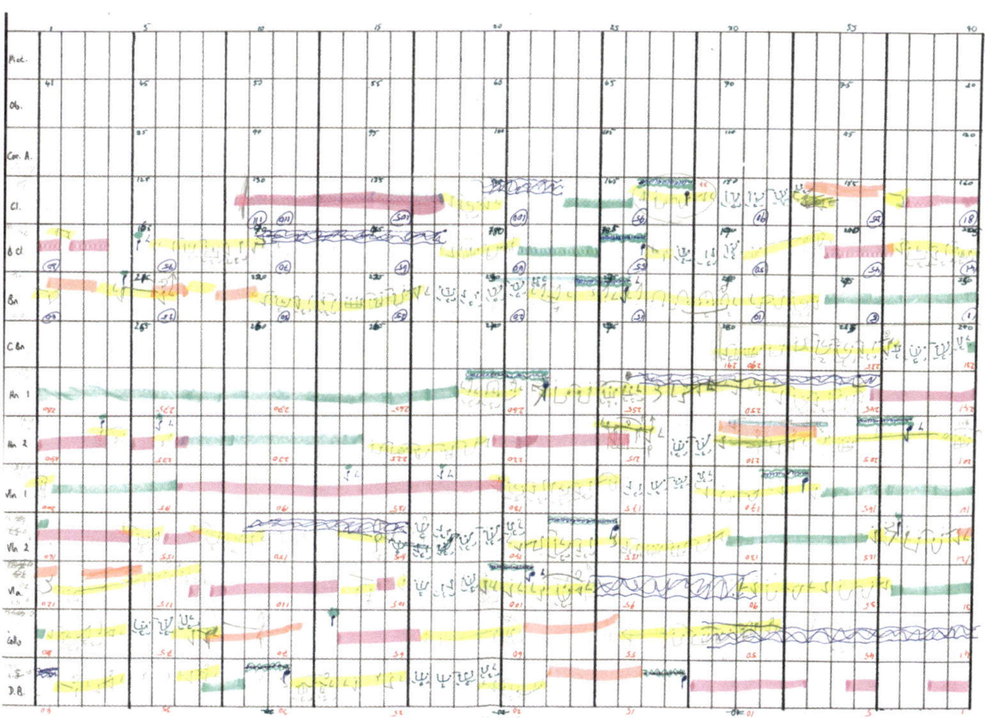

Kāea – *more plotting.*

Alas! How Swift for trumpet and chamber orchestra, was commissioned in 2006 by the New Zealand Symphony Orchestra for their Principal Trumpet, Michael Kirgan. In the garden of Inverleith Park Edinburgh there is a sundial. The inscription on the north face says, 'I number none but sunny hours.' On the south side it says 'So passes life. Alas! How swift.' The music is fast, with a constant speed of 138 beats per minute. Around this underlying tempo the speed sometimes quickens and sometimes slows.

Stan Pritchard / Alamy Stock Photo

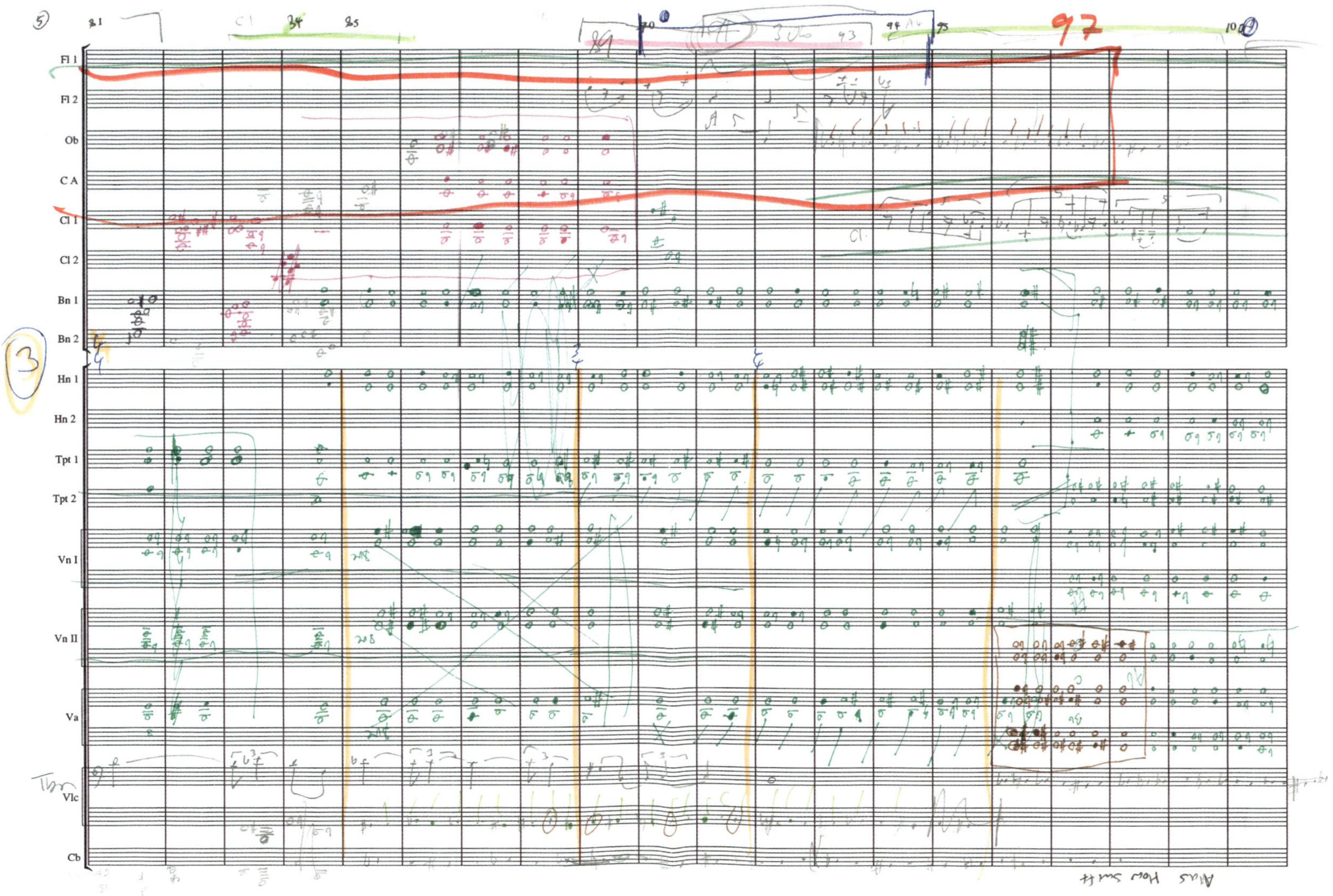

Fl 1
Fl 2
Ob
C A
Cl 1
Cl 2
Bn 1
Bn 2
Hn 1
Hn 2
Tpt 1
Tpt 2
Vn I
Vn II
Va
Vlc
Cb

Alas! How swift – *harmonic preparation.*

Perhaps all these plans and calculations are a game. Making them up can be enjoyable and even another form of procrastination, but once the rules are established the hard work begins. Self-imposed rules allow complete freedom of expression while keeping a check on self-indulgence.

In 2015 I was commissioned by the Scottish Chamber Orchestra to write a clarinet concerto, *Llanto,* for Spanish clarinettist Maximiliano Martín. In 2019 he commissioned a clarinet quintet, *Rima,* the title of which means 'five' in te reo Māori and 'rhyme' in Italian, Spanish and other languages. *Rima* is an attempt to find affinities between two very different and refined vocal traditions – Māori chant and Scottish Gaelic psalm singing. With the Covid-19 pandemic the first performance had to be delayed.

Rima – *jottings.*

Chapter 5
Wednesday 13 October 1944

> 'Take my camel, dear,' said my Aunt Dot, as she climbed down from this animal on her return from High Mass.
>
> *Rose Macaulay*, The Towers of Trebizond

I was born on Wednesday 13 October 1944 in a tent. My earliest sensory memory is the sweet, reassuring smell of fresh warm camel dung. I was weaned on camel milk and my young ears were tickled with the sound of the qanun, the ney and the sistrum.

My maternal grandfather is thought by some to have been T.E. Lawrence. It is claimed that he was seduced in a tent in the Wadi Zin wilderness by an aberrant Scottish Free Church missionary called Morag. Gossip and obloquy surrounded her. Still in the early stages of pregnancy, Morag fled through the desert to Kuwait. There she boarded a merchant vessel bound for the tiny port of Dubai. In Dubai she was welcomed and looked after by a group of hospitable and sympathetic Bedouins, who cared for her abandoned daughter when she fled back to the bosom of her family in Glasgow.

Morag's daughter Muriel was not only conceived but also born and raised in a tent. When she was a young woman, Muriel went to work in a small pearl trading company in Dubai. There she met and married the accountant, Jack Cresswell – a caring but taciturn New Zealander with a fascination for tortoises. How Jack came to be there is a mystery shrouded in secrecy and suspicion. Any attempts to ask him about his past were met with obfuscation or total silence. To this day we have no explanation. There are however, rumours of a Jac Cresyndda involved in dodgy accounting in the coal mines of the Rhymney Valley in South Wales in the early 1930s.

With the 1930s depression and the advent of cultured pearls, the pearl trade languished and finally collapsed. In 1947 Muriel and Jack packed up and the family made its way to New Zealand leaving behind six tortoises, two ostriches and a pet zebra.

All through my childhood in our suburban housing estate house, I yearned for a pet camel with its symphony of colours. Nothing could have pleased me more than to tend it, watch it lollop around our hillside back garden and let it sleep in the warmth of the kitchen. I would have loved to take it to school for my morning talk.

Jack and Muriel were pillars of the local Gilbert and Sullivan Society. They would go out some winter evenings, in their camel-hair coats, to warble through *HMS Pinafore, The Pirates of Penzance* or *The Gondoliers.*

I was sent to the nearby convent for piano lessons where I pounded the instrument mercilessly and drove my teacher, a nun, to despair. She harangued my parents and told them that I should never be allowed near a piano again. I never looked back – my musical career was born. I still think of those camels and hanker for one to carry my shopping.

I was born on Thursday 13 October 1944 in a tent. My earliest sensory memory is the sweet, reassuring smell of fresh warm camel dung. I was weaned on camel milk and my young ears were tickled with the sound of the qanun, the ney and the sistrum.

Every summer, immediately after Christmas, we packed the trailer with summer clothes, tinned food, camp chairs, stretcher beds, sleeping bags, lilos, camp tables and tent and set off on holiday. We covered the country, staying in campsites from Kaitaia to Invercargill. Favourite sites were Rainbow Springs in Rotorua and Redwood Park near Auckland.

The tent made of thick green canvas was known as the 'poleless tent'. In fact it required 18 wooden poles and many wooden pegs, but there was no centre pole. Instead, four poles put together with springs in the middle were inserted into holes at the top of the main corner poles and into a dome at the apex. My mother's brother Uncle Richard usually came with us. He had a poleless inflatable igloo tent. It quickly developed a leak and had to be propped up with a spare pole.

The 'poleless' tent, Mercury Bay, 1953.

My maternal grandfather is thought by some to have been T.E. Lawrence. It is claimed that he was seduced in a tent in the Wadi Zin wilderness by an aberrant Scottish Free Church missionary called Morag. Gossip and obloquy surrounded her. Still in the early stages of pregnancy, Morag fled through the desert to Kuwait. There she boarded a merchant vessel bound for the tiny port of Dubai. In Dubai she was welcomed and looked after by a group of hospitable and sympathetic Bedouins, who cared for her abandoned daughter when she fled back to the bosom of her family in Glasgow.

My maternal grandfather was not T.E. Lawrence. There are no family connections with either Glasgow or the Free Church of Scotland. However during the heatwave and drought of 1976, which brought record temperatures and swarms of ladybirds to the United Kingdom, we moved from Aberdeen to Glasgow where we found accommodation in the potting shed of the honorary Greek consul's house. There was one room with an alcove for the bed and a spartan bathroom. In the warmth and sunlight of that summer and with a lovely garden it looked charming, but in the winter it turned dark and clammy – pink fungus growing on the walls, phantom dripping, scuttling creatures, a creaking roof, flickering lights and questionable wiring were all somewhat irksome. From there we moved into the home of an academic who went away on sabbatical leave.

My stand-in work at Glasgow University involved various bits and pieces of teaching. The most rewarding was a lively class for contemporary music studies. One of the students, Iain Matheson, became a firm and helpful friend with a keen eye for proof-reading. The Glasgow community of composers in the 1970s was welcoming, hospitable and supportive. It included Thomas Wilson, Malcolm Rayment, John Maxwell Geddes, Edward McGuire and William Sweeney.

Composers in Glasgow for the 1993 launch of two CDs by the Paragon Ensemble – me, Thomas Wilson, William Sweeney, Philip Norris, Edward McGuire and James MacMillan.

My orchestral work *Salm* was written in Glasgow in 1977 and the following year it won the Ian Whyte Award. The award was given by a private donor through the Scottish National Orchestra Society to honour the memory of Ian Whyte, composer, conductor and founder of the BBC Scottish Symphony Orchestra. At the time it was the most prestigious award in the United Kingdom for British or British-resident composers under 35.

The *P* in the title of *Salm* is not only silent, but also invisible – it is the Gaelic spelling. *Salm* is based on the practice of psalm singing by Gaelic-speaking congregations, mainly in the Western Highlands and Islands of Scotland. Most of the tunes were introduced from

Discussing the score of Salm *with Italian conductor Piero Gamba when the New Zealand Symphony Orchestra gave the New Zealand premiere in July 1979.* Stuff Ltd

Europe at the time of the Reformation (c.1525–1560), but the style of singing them was derived from the Scottish musical tradition – the same tradition that can be seen in the pìobaireachd. The psalm tunes with texts were not printed until more than 100 years after the Reformation, by which time all the processes which occur in the oral transmission of music began to operate. The tunes, which were originally in an idiom quite foreign to the Highlanders, soon began to develop a character all of their own. Two innovations in particular were important in the evolution of the style – the part played by the precentor and the use of ornamentation.

Illiteracy, and the scarcity of printed texts for those who could read, led to the introduction of the precentor. The minister reads the psalm, the precentor (who may also be the minister) sings the first few lines and the members of the congregation gradually join as they recognise the tune. They sing unaccompanied and in unison with the precentor embellishing every note as the spirit moves. Ornamentation of the tune is developed to such an extent that each syllable has its own melisma and the length of the tunes increases so that they become very far removed from the original. Members of the congregation improvise their own embellishments. The effect is unique – a long strong tune comes through a maze of sound something like a Celtic knot pattern.

Celtic knot patterns.

This method of psalm singing suggested a whole compositional method. Instead of taking one of the traditional tunes I made up my own in the same style, with four clearly related phrases. Both movements of *Salm* are based on this tune.

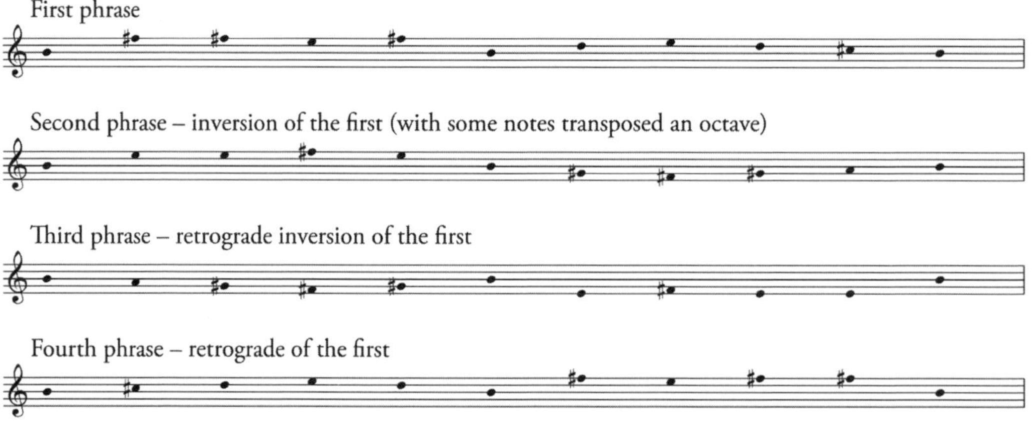

With the ornamentation and stretched notes it becomes this – beginning with the solo cello and moving into divided cellos.

f
8
14
mf
21
3
25
mp
30
A
mf
f
3
33

The solo cello acts as the precentor, beginning the first movement and gradually leading the whole orchestra into the psalm. The tune becomes more and more heavily ornamented as the movement grows. In the second complementary movement the tune is less obvious, but more vigorously embellished. An ironic touch towards the end is the introduction of a tune in the piccolo and high violins suggesting the rather sinister protestant flute bands of Northern Ireland and Glasgow.

At the end of the first movement at the first performance in the Music Hall in Aberdeen on 30 January 1979 I heard a voice behind me say 'gorgeous'. I don't know what the voice thought of the second movement.

My ticket for the first performance of Salm.

This was the first time an orchestral work of mine was played in a concert. My only previous experience was in the recording studio with the New Zealand Symphony Orchestra when they recorded my early violin concerto with Alex Lindsay as soloist and Edwin Carr conducting. I was too scared to go to the recording at first and only turned up when they were half-way through.

Salm received the second highest number of votes from delegates attending the 1981 UNESCO International Rostrum of Composers[1] as did my *Concerto for Cello and Orchestra* in 1988.

In October 2003 we were invited by the Gaelic singer/songwriter, Calum Martin to a recording project he was organising in the Free Church at Back (Am Bac) near Stornoway on the Isle of Lewis. All the psalms in the repertoire were recorded to make a permanent archive of Gaelic psalm singing. A large congregation gathered for the first

For several years the Concert Programme (now RNZ Concert) sent me to the Rostrum as the New Zealand delegate.

session on Monday evening in the stern, grey, bleak and forbidding roughcast building. Before the proceedings began we sat on hard wooden pews in complete silence. The women wore hats and the men dark suits and ties. Once the singing began, the whole building trembled with fierce devotion and God-fearing fervour. After the first recording session there was a sedate cup of tea, served in white porcelain cups with school cake and fern tartlets for everyone in the church hall. We asked two Free Church ministers if they thought women would ever be able to act as precentors in a service. One was open to the idea, but the other, a particularly severe individual, shook his head and said slowly, 'Oo no, no, no.' It seems that women are allowed to do this only if there is no capable man present. Before we all left, the minister of Back Church said, 'We have had a lovely session tonight. There will be another one tomorrow, so please ask all your friends to come and join us – the more the merrier.'

In choosing to use folk music for the foundation of a composition, composers are seeking some common ground between themselves and a group of people in order to communicate their own ideas and feelings. Folk music is often an ordering of sound according to certain patterns which have evolved as an aid to human actions for rituals, working, dancing, playing games and so on – so composers who base their work on folk music are looking to communicate their own ideas with their audience in terms of comprehensible human actions.

Morag's daughter Muriel was not only conceived but also born and raised in a tent. When she was a young woman Muriel went to work in a small pearl trading company in Dubai. There she met and married the accountant, Jack Cresswell – a caring but taciturn New Zealander with a fascination for tortoises.

Tortoises are reclusive creatures with hard carapaces – attributes necessary for a composer.

How Jack came to be there is a mystery shrouded in secrecy and suspicion. Any attempts to ask him about his past were met with obfuscation or total silence. To this day we have no explanation. There are however, rumours of a Jac Cresyndda involved in dodgy accounting in the coal mines of the Rhymney Valley, South Wales in the early 1930s.

Early in 1978 I was encouraged to apply for the position of Music Organiser at Chapter Arts Centre in Cardiff. Catherine was happy in her work at Clydebank library, but after much consideration I applied and was appointed to start on 1 April 1978.

Chapter Arts Centre, housed in an old school in the Canton district of Cardiff, comprised two cinemas, an art gallery, a theatre, restaurant, bar and studios for painters, sculptors, film makers, actors, writers and a violin maker. It was dedicated to new and experimental work in all fields of the arts. My job was to organise concerts of contemporary music with a wide range of visiting soloists and ensembles, folk music and jazz as well as fostering various types of workshops, mostly involving improvisation.

Chapter Arts Centre was established in 1971, and is still an international centre for contemporary arts and culture.

We worked closely with a group of players from the BBC Welsh Symphony Orchestra commissioning works from Welsh composers. Catherine found library work, first in the School of Architecture in the University of Wales Institute of Technology and then in the periodicals department.

For one concert I indulged in a weakness I had at the time and made an arrangement of two Sousa marches, *The Washington Post* and *The High School Cadets*. This did not go down well with the new music purists. A third march, *The Royal Welch Fusiliers (No. 3),* was also included.

In 1929, 50 years earlier, Sousa composed *The Royal Welch Fusiliers* in honour of the eponymous regiment and the following year rewrote it. The two versions are known as *The Royal Welch Fusiliers (No. 1)* and *The Royal Welch Fusiliers (No. 2).*

My drawing of John Philip Sousa.

I created a third bogus version – the conductor and players were none the wiser and the announcements for broadcasts were deadpan. The march is based on *Sosban Fach*, meaning 'little saucepan', a nonsensical Welsh folk song about a pressurised housewife. The words, written in the 1870s, are thought to have come from the Welsh bard Richard Davies or Mynydogg, and the tune was written by the Reverend D.M. Davies a few years later. The song is often heard ringing around rugby grounds, especially in Llanelli.

Mae bys Meri-Ann wedi brifo,
A Dafydd y gwas ddim yn iach.
Mae'r baban yn y crud yn crio,
A'r gath wedi sgramo Joni bach.
Sosban fach yn berwi ar y tân,
Sosban fawr yn berwi ar y llawr,
A'r gath wedi sgramo Joni bach.

Mary-Ann has hurt her finger,
And David the servant isn't well.
The baby in the cradle is crying,
And the cat has scratched little Johnny.
A little saucepan is boiling on the fire,
A little saucepan is boiling on the floor,
And the cat has scratched little Johnny.

A parody became popular at Welsh rugby grounds after 1972.

Who beat the All Blacks,
Who beat the All Blacks,
Who beat the All Blacks?
Good old Sosban fach.

It must be said that Sousa's novel *The Fifth String*, in which a virtuoso violinist adds a mysterious fifth string to his violin in order to win the heart of his beloved Mildred, is no literary masterpiece.

Above and opposite: from The Royal Welch Fusiliers (No. 3).[2]

9
Picc.
Ob.
Cl.
B. Cl.
Bsn.
Hn.
Tpt.
Tbn.
Db.
pizz.
22
1.
2.
arco
33

Administrative work involves coping with tedious minutiae, proliferating jargon, form-filling, meetings and self-perpetuating bureaucracy. I began to feel uncomfortable and frustrated at Chapter and at a planning meeting in February 1980 I resigned on the spur of the moment. Planners and implementers are necessary, but the byzantine world of arts administration was not for me. I saw an advertisement in the Western Mail for a trainee banana ripener[3] and, tempting though it was, I did not apply.

During the two years in Cardiff I found time to write just three works that matter – *The Magical Wooden Head* for strings, brass and percussion, which won the Dunedin Civic Orchestra Prize in 1980, *Prayer for the cure of a sprained back* for solo soprano, and *Hocket* for bass clarinet and tape delay system. *Prayer for the cure of a sprained back* was written for the English soprano Jane Manning, who gave many exquisite performances of it.

The first endeavours to write a history of New Zealand were made by Arthur Saunders Thomson MD, Surgeon-General 58th (Rutlandshire) Regiment of Foot, in the 1850s. Saunders was born in Arbroath in 1816 and studied medicine in Edinburgh. He died in China in 1860, where he was in charge of a medical supply ship and was buried in the Russian cemetery in Beijing. *The Story of New Zealand* published in 1859 contained pastiche Māori poetry as well as some attempts at translation such as this prayer for the cure of a sprained back.

Close up your bones;
Close up your blood;
Close up your joints;
The sky will assist thee to close,
And the earth will become bones for thee.

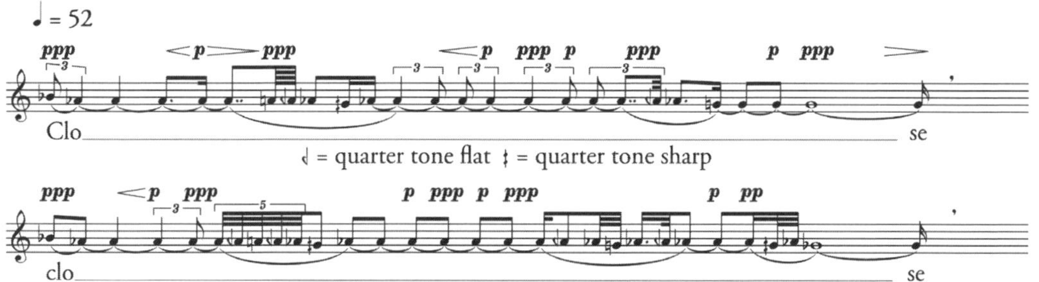

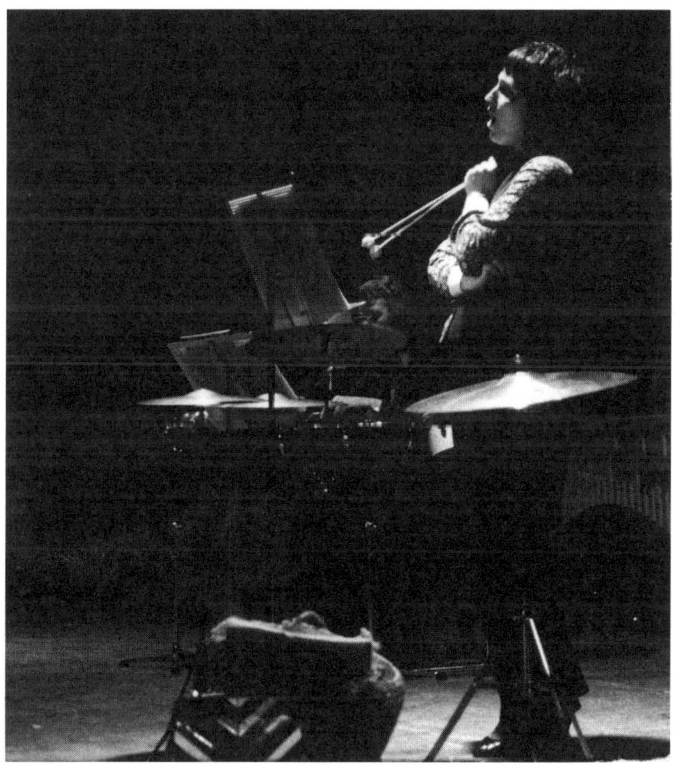

Jane Manning (1938–2021) premiered more than 350 works and, with her husband Anthony Payne was a life-long supporter of contemporary composers and performers. Dominic Saunders

Harry Sparnaay, the virtuoso Dutch bass clarinet player, gave a concert at Chapter Arts Centre and we became friends. He commissioned two works from me – *Hocket* and later, in 1982, *Le Sucre du Printemps* for six bass clarinets and three contrabass clarinets. The music comes from some treacly fragments of the bass clarinet part of Stravinsky's *Le Sacre du Printemps*. In the programme for the first performance by the Bass Clarinet Collective there was an error. The crucial letter change was overlooked.

From Cardiff we moved to Edinburgh, but not before making some important and lasting friendships. Two of these, Veronica Porter and Tim Thornicroft, have been very helpful in preparing this memoir. Another was an ebullient serial vice-chancellor, Mike Thorne.

With the 1930s depression and the advent of cultured pearl,s the pearl trade languished and finally collapsed. In 1947 Muriel and Jack packed up and the family made its way to New Zealand leaving behind six tortoises, two ostriches and a pet zebra.

The ostrich has keen eyesight, but poor senses of smell and hearing.
The zebra has weak eyesight, but acute senses of smell and hearing.
The ostrich is dim-sighted, but has sharp senses of smell and hearing.
The zebra is eagle-eyed, but has delicate senses of smell and hearing.
The ostrich has wonderful senses of sight, smell and hearing.
The zebra has outstanding senses of sight, smell and hearing.

Whatever the truth of these various hypotheses may be, ostriches and zebras do seek each other's company and roam around together warning each other of the presence of predators.

There can be confusion in the importance of roles in collaborative work, which can lead to difficulties and egotistical issues. Most of the collaborations that I have been involved in have been enjoyable and uncomplicated because they have been carried out with mutual respect and understanding. Two writers that I have a close and happy relationship and friendship with are Fiona Farrell in New Zealand and Ron Butlin in Scotland. Both are happy to make any changes I might ask for. Neither of them ever asks me to change the notes, but they make suggestions about form or interpretation.

Ron tells of getting a phone call one day when we were writing a chamber opera asking for, 'a few lines of deep despair and a bawdy, drunken song'.

Ron Butlin. Regi Claire

In 2013 the New Zealand Symphony Orchestra commissioned me to write a work referring to the Christchurch earthquake. I was very keen to write a song-cycle for baritone and orchestra with short poems by Fiona Farrell. We decided to take a broader view than just the Christchurch earthquakes and Fiona came up with perfect poems to set. In the programme note for *The Clock Stops* she wrote:

> These songs are about the history of cities: from swamp to Çatal Hüyük where the dead lie buried by the kitchen hearth, to office block and freeway. The most spectacular of human artefacts, they are organic creations subject to time and to destruction by human and natural forces.

The Clock Stops

1 Fog
The bird sings. Three
notes. Over. And over.
And the city rises
through fog
like a woman waking.

2 Hīnaki (eel-pot)
Hīnaki in creek,
fish weaving the water,
voices weaving
the crackle of flax.

3 Map
We tacked the streets flat
on a map back in Clapham.
Grab. Snap.
Flag flap.
Chop. Hack
Stack. Sack.
Sheep's back.
Mudflat to tramtrack.

4 Lullabye
Sleep little bird
in your broken nest.
Rocked by storm,
safe from harm.
The moon soothes the city.
The wind sings from the west.
See.
Saw.
See.
Saw.
Hush.
Hush.

5 Wings
We flew to the city on
white wings. Perched
like birds on clinking
shingle

6 Downtown
Hammer clatter
tower block
café chatter
parking lot
office showroom
movie theatre
bar brothel
bank stock
factory office
mall cathedral
hospital and
shop shop shop
No Right Turn
No Left Turn
Traffic merging
Give Way
STOP

7 We built a city
We built a city.
It rocked.
It rolled.

8 Lament
The bird sings
on a broken wall.
Cities rise.
Cities fall.
The bird sings
on a broken wall
So it goes.

La la
So it goes.
La la la

9 Jericho

We circled the city
and at the seventh trump
the walls fell.
At the seventh trump
the clock stopped.
The dog barked.
The clothesline hopped.
The window cracked.
The road jumped.
The walls fell down flat,
and we stumbled out,
mumbling.

10 Skater

The young men ride
the rubble. Slide down
its broken balustrades,
flip from its walls, skid
across its buried cars
and leap its cracks.

11 Çatal Hüyük

In the city the dead lie
buried beneath the kitchens.
Their ashes sit on the
mantelpiece, next the clock.
Tick.
Tock.

Fiona Farrell

All the music in this song-cycle springs, in one way or another, from the words. In any setting of words, the structure and character of the music are governed by them. Monteverdi was attacked for his treatment of dissonance and his modernist approach to composition. In response he said that the text should command the music – and the words should be the mistress of the harmony.

Writing words for music is a very particular art. The text can't have the density of poetry or the expanse of prose and must be very clear, short and direct. The words dictate the rhythm and inflexion, so too many words make for tedious music.

The pitches and rhythms in these 11 short songs arise directly from the words. Every word commands its own pitch and rhythm and it's my job to prise these out. The resulting musical ideas are then unfolded and embellished by the orchestra either as an accompaniment, an elaboration or a contrasting point of view. The character of the music is determined by an emotional response to these poems.

Setting words is a different way of working. The approach to an orchestral piece or a piece for string quartet is pretty much the same, but setting words demands something else. The feeling and the structure are determined for the composer – but the task is to find out what these things are.

In *The Voice Inside*, seven settings of poems by Ron Butlin relating to the violin, I have taken the same approach as with *The Clock Stops*. It is a concerto for violin, soprano and orchestra, and was commissioned for the BBC Scottish Symphony Orchestra's 'Strings Attached' series in 2002. After talking with Ron about tonal inflexions, rhythms, vowels, form and music in general, he wrote seven short and wonderfully apt poems. I only needed to ask for one or two small changes of rhythm and the occasional vowel sound.

The Voice Inside

1 Invocation
Hush – hush –
Hush the strings –
Hush the body –
Still the bow to silence
echoing the silence long before
the strings, the body and the bow.
Before the strings were laid in place,
pegged and tied,
stretched and tightened taut.
Then arched above emptiness into the emptiness all around,
that held the greater silence
long before, the echo of the greatest silence
ever.

Then touch – hush – touch – hush
Touch . . . Stroke to sound – draw sound
out of tightness, out of stillness, out of emptiness,
giving shape to the emptiness that everything
comes from and returns to. Giving scale
to the emptiness. Giving voice, giving life.

2 Scherzo I
Your voice / My voice
Sound plaited with sound
Silence layered upon silence
criss-crossing, parting,
sliding together
to harmonise,

And O, those fugal lines
of tig and catch,
touch and snatch,
tag and miss.
Catch as catch can
boy and girl, woman, man
contrapuntal, asymptotic
palindromic
mirrorwise inversion
canonic imitation
Your theme or mine?
Line for line
into the bars
and out.
Your key or mine?
– let's intertwine.

3 Vigorous
Not a woman's voice – no:
Hard and harshness
to kiss. Stride and strident
Not a woman's voice – no:
Slash, strike, cut, score
Not pleading, not pleasing, not –
Wound to the heart.
Stab to the soul.
Scar, scrape, mark, march
Destroy, destroy, destroy.
Command and order.
Design and structure
Pattern and plan.
Man – forming everything around him
Man – controlling everything around him
light and darkness.

4 Slow Movement
All sound has always held itself as absence
– in heart of strings, in hollowed body,
and unstrung bow – and as presence.
Soul as silence.

5 Scherzo II
Four strings, body and bow.
Locatelli, Corelli,
Paganini, Tartini,
Niel Gow, Niel Gow, Niel Gow.

Four strings, body and bow.
Guarneri, Amati,
Stradivari, Viotti,
Vivaldi, Grapelli,
Spohr, Spivakovsky,
Niel Gow, Niel Gow, Niel Gow.

6 Burlesque
Twelve equal tones dangling on a score,
if one of them should modulate
– would there be a melody
where none had been before?

Twelve equal tones dangling on a stave,
if all of them should modulate
– which one would we save?
Chaos comes but once a year,
creation's always late
so choose the note you like to hear
– the rest will sublimate.

7 Plea

Hear my voice, hear me listening
to the voice inside,
so deep, deep inside:
trembling, stirring – fear and hope,
awakening love, awakening hatred,
emerging – longing and desire.

Rising up from the core of the earth it feels,
from the furthest rim of the farthest star it feels,
from the darkest hour, the darkest night
the radiant sun at noon
– into my heart, into my lungs, my throat.

Revealing what I did not know.
Expressing what I dare not feel.
Saying what cannot keep silent.

Ron Butlin

Other collaborations with Ron include four small-scale operas: *Good Angel Bad Angel*, *The Perfect Woman*, *The Money Man* and *Wedlock*.

I have worked briefly and agreeably with some other writers: C.K. Stead for *Words for Music* which was commissioned for the 1990 Waitangi Day service in Westminster Abbey, Marco Bucchieri for *Tre Canti* and *Il Suono di Enormi Distanze*, and my sister-in-law Mary Cresswell, who wrote *Das Lied von dem Fisch*.

On the morning of 2 January 2015 I heard a compelling news item on the radio. There was an interview with a vet who had just carried out an hour long operation on a constipated goldfish. She said, 'He had a lump blocking his bottom.' I sent the internet reference of this story to Mary and by return email she sent the first poem. The other poems followed.

Das Lied von dem Fisch

1 Vet operates on constipated goldfish
aber man kann nie wissen
ob die Fische pissen

2 crappie bass
crappie bass
and bluefish
patagonian toothfish
but trout
are
out

3 shark-suckers
shark-suckers spill from the marlin's gill
but not when the whiting are biting
pelagic
and
tragic

4 we were profound
we were profound
now we are gone
fish with a tooth
soup of your youth
we only bemoan
Patagonia

5 in diesen Hallen
in diesen Hallen
Fisch gefallen
mische tische
gefilte Fishe

6 fanfare for the order of the garter
oni soit qui halibut

7 kennst du das Glas
kennst du das Glas
wo die Fische poopen?
bloop
bloop
bloopen
fischenpoopen
a-a
a-a
a-a
aaaaaaaaaaaaaaaaaaa

Mary Cresswell

All through my childhood in our suburban housing estate house, I yearned for a pet camel with its symphony of colours. Nothing could have pleased me more than to tend it, watch it lollop around our hillside back garden and let it sleep in the warmth of the kitchen.

We were never allowed pets when we were children.

I would have loved to take it to school for my morning talk

One evening, when I was five or six, we were taken to a performance of *The Pirates of Penzance,* most of which I slept through. When it came to the morning talk next day I put my hand up and said that I would sing a pirate song. As soon as I found myself alone facing the whole class I became dumbstruck, wiggled a loose tooth and sat down.

Jack and Muriel were pillars of the local Gilbert and Sullivan Society. They would go out some winter evenings in their camel-hair coats, to warble through HMS Pinafore, The Pirates of Penzance *or* The Gondoliers.

My brother Max was very enthusiastic about Gilbert and Sullivan, and bought all the records he could find of the operas. Frequently the sound of this music wafted through the house. Whenever the J. C. Williamson Gilbert and Sullivan Opera Company toured from Australia, or the Wellington Gilbert and Sullivan Society mounted a production, we were all taken to see it. To this day warblings from these operas can be heard coming from Max.

I was sent to the nearby convent for piano lessons where I pounded the instrument mercilessly and drove my teacher, a nun, to despair. She harangued my parents and told them that I should never be allowed near a piano again. I never looked back – my musical career was born. I still think of those camels and hanker for one to carry my shopping.

John Thompson's *Modern Course for the Piano,* published in the 1940s, was used by generations of music teachers. My piano teacher Miss Fahey taught in a little cabin beside St Teresa's Catholic Church in Karori. The first book she gave me was John Thompson's *Teaching Little Fingers to Play.* My favourite pieces in this collection were: 'Song of the Volga Boatmen', 'Steam-boat Round the Bend', 'Blue-Bells of Scotland', 'Flying to the Moon' and 'From a Wigwam'. All these pieces transported me to a far-off place, but my piano playing did not improve. It left Miss Fahey in despair until one day I surprised her with a fluid and enthusiastic rendering of 'The Sailor's Hornpipe'. Her despair soon returned.

Intermezzo 2
Cats

Equo ne credite
Don't trust the horse
Virgil, The Aeneid, *Book 2*

Cats are very important. Our three cats have all been black and white with black noses. The first was given to us in 1983 when he was three or four weeks old. He could stand on the palm of my hand and fit into a brown paper bag. We were told that he was female and decided to call him Victoria because my sister-in-law in Wellington had a cat called Albert. When we discovered that he was a male cat we changed the name to Victor Emmanuel or more properly, Vittorio Emanuele. He soon became known as Manuel.

He used to sit on the desk to help me with my work and had the uncanny knack of always sitting on the piece of paper that I would require next.

Victor Emmanuel 1983–2002, painted by Richard N. Russell.

Vittorio Emanuele II supported the unification of Italy and became its first king. He was popularly known as 'Il Re Galantuomo' – the gentleman king and 'Padre della Patria' – father of the fatherland. The name seemed particularly appropriate since Victor Emmanuel II was fundamentally pleasure seeking.

Victor Emmanuel's successor, Victoria de los Angeles had an artistic temperament. Some visitors to our apartment were petrified and went to great lengths to avoid going near her, but she was very beautiful.

Victoria 2002–2013.

After Victoria came Pomponazzo, commonly known as Pompey.

Pomponazzo 2011–2021, painted by Richard N. Russell.

In Mantua there is a beautiful little theatre designed by Antonio Bibiena. The building, otherwise known as the Teatro Scientifico or the Teatro dell'Accademia, was completed on 3 December 1769 and on 16 January 1770 the 14-year-old Wolfgang Amadeus Mozart gave a recital in the theatre. His father Leopold described it in a letter to his wife as the most beautiful theatre in the world.

Standing in two niches in the wall at the back of the stage are statues of Virgil and Pomponazzo. Who is Pomponazzo? We asked our Italian friends and they shook their heads.

Pietro Pomponazzo was born in Mantua on 16 September 1462 and died in Bologna on 18 March 1525. He studied medicine and philosophy at the University of Padua before taking teaching posts in Ferrara and Bologna. Edith Templeton, author of raunchy novels, describes him in *The Surprise of Cremona* as 'the greatest Aristotelian philosopher of his day'. Pomponazzo got into trouble with the church for his writings on the immortality of the soul, but asserted his loyalty and was not tried for heresy.

Perhaps it is the way the name rolls off the tongue that appealed.

When Catherine and I lived at the Lilburn House in Wellington during 2006–07 we had to 'make do' with our neighbour Charlotte Wilson's tabby called Pippen.
Alan Knowles

Chapter 6
Thursday 13 October 1944

Io parlo parlo, dice Marco, ma chi mi
ascolta richiede solo le parole che aspetta.
I speak I speak, says Marco, but whoever listens
to me takes in only the words he is expecting.
Italo Calvino, 'Le città invisibili' *IX*

I was born in Wellington, New Zealand on Thursday 13 October 1944 to Italian immigrant parents. My father had been a priest in the beautiful baroque city of Lecce in Puglia. His name was Giacomo Pozzo di Crescione.

With his soaring tenor voice Giacomo longed to become known as Il Sacredote di Canto – the singing priest. The honeyed tones of his alluring voice penetrated the thick limestone walls of Il Convento Faggiano where an impressionable novice, Mariella Aguzzo prayed and hung on every note. In the balmy summer evenings, with the delicate fragrance of olive blossoms and a glass of primitivo from the Abbey of Santa Maria di Cerrutti, Mariella, with a keen ear for music, gave herself freely to tears of joy at the sound of that voice.

To cut a long story short they met by chance at the Porta Napoli. Giacomo, entranced by Mariella's beauty, could not stop himself from bursting into Puccini's great love song 'Ti amo'. Mariella, captivated, swooned. He swept her up and carried her to the nearest hotel and there, it seems, I was conceived. Quickly they became the talk of the monasteries and convents of Puglia and beyond. For some it was a chink of light in war-torn Italy, but for others a monumental sin and scandal. In disgrace and with the power of the church on their tails they decided to flee the country. Finding sympathetic ears in an American bomber group stationed in Lecce, they were whisked away to begin their journey to the other side of the world.

In New Zealand Giacomo and Mariella anglicised their names and became Jack Cresswell and Muriel Sharp. They forswore the demon primitivo, renounced Catholicism, joined the Salvation Army and were married in Wellington. Mariella/Muriel gave birth to me in the Salvation Army hospital for unmarried mothers. Refusing to speak Italian ever again, they quickly became assimilated and learned to obliterate all trace of their mother tongue. I was brought up without a word of Italian, but with the clandestine rosary in one hand and the booming bass drum in the other.

Jack and Muriel were determined to nurture me in a musical environment. Early attempts to teach me to play the mandolin failed. With the mouth organ things only improved slightly, but then I was thrown into the brass band and took to it like a duck to water. My real pleasure however came from listening to the band music and writing down musical patterns. As a form of teenage rebellion I toyed with the possibility of entering the priesthood, but this was roundly discouraged. Only in later life did I discover that I was Giacomo's third son.

I was born in Wellington, New Zealand on Wednesday 13 October 1944 to Italian immigrant parents. My father had been a priest in the beautiful baroque city of Lecce in Puglia. His name was Giacomo Pozzo di Crescione.

My links with Italy came much later. When someone assures you that you will get on well with one of their friends it doesn't usually bode well. However, in the case of the Bolognese painter Maurizio Bottarelli this assurance proved to be right. Bottarelli and his wife Angela came to stay with us during the 1984 Edinburgh Festival at the suggestion of a Scottish friend Elspeth Fehilly, who knew Maurizio's cousin. It quickly became clear that we shared a similar artistic outlook and a deep friendship began.

Over the years we have taken many a glass of wine or whisky together in the atmospheric old osterie of Bologna, where vecchietti sit around wooden tables playing cards and talking politics, intellettuali gather and soliloquise, or join in arcane and increasingly befuddled conversations, cognoscenti air their superior expertise to all those within range, and young artists mingle respectfully with their elders to discuss materials, techniques and concepts – all huddling in groups in quiet dark corners or spilling out loudly on to the street.

With Maurizio near Bologna.

Maurizio taught at L'Accademia di Brera in Milan and L'Accademia di Belle Arti in Bologna. He was a very fine and popular teacher. I saw this when on several occasions he asked me to come and talk to his students in both Milan and Bologna.

Composers examine the world through their ears, just as painters examine it through their eyes. Their ears and eyes nourish their emotions, but their investigations have to have the same seriousness of purpose as any scientific inquiry. They examine the relationship between abstract beauty (the coupling of pitch and rhythm, or the play of light and colour) and the world of the emotions. Every detail has to be considered and stored in the mind, only later to be realised on paper or canvas.

When we look at a painting, a still-life or a landscape, we look for something deep and private, something about art and something about ourselves. If we find what we are looking for we realise that no attempt to put it into words is adequate.

We can taste and smell Cézanne's apples and peaches, we can be soaked by Hiroshige's sudden showers, we can be churned up in Jackson Pollock's whirlpools, or we can become lost in the hills of Colin McCahon's Otago landscapes, but we can't accurately describe the excitement of these combined sensations and any attempt to explain them can only be very approximate. We appreciate these images only when we convert them into the terms of our own moods and sensitivities. What concerns art is what we feel, not just what we know.

Landscape can have many deep and mysterious qualities. Artists have to assimilate it rather than simply making it a point of reference. It has to pass through the filter of memory and be clarified in the artist's mind. It becomes at once distanced and personalised. The landscape becomes locked in a struggle with the artist and takes over the soul. Artists can't be afraid of revealing themselves in their work because this struggle is an encounter with their own vision of the world and their inner landscape. Through landscape, artists find a way of using natural forces to convey their expressive vision. The confrontations and the harmony within the landscape can become a metaphor for human conflict and aspirations.

The musical score is a map; a map made by charting what is already there – the inner landscape. It is a map that charts fault lines, a map that marks out events, reveals secrets and tells stories. It is not a perfect map, like that in Borges' short story 'On Exactitude in Science on a scale of 1:1', but a map that attempts to take us beyond the frustration of words. The score is an exact chart, with a grid showing precise locations and pinpointing special features in the landscape; but the map also depicts a landscape and plots a path through the emotional ties to human existence within that landscape.

Maurizio, Mimmo to his friends, and Angela visited New Zealand in March 2007 when we were resident in the Lilburn House and we drove all over to show them the country.

At Lyell on the west coast of the South Island, where a small town once stood.

Mimmo on the ferry to Waiheke Island, 2007. Angela Peluso

As raw material for his work Mimmo was not interested in beautiful or spectacular landscapes, but the black sands at Mōkau on the north Taranaki coast caught his imagination. Looking down on the incoming tide he saw lace-like patterns in the white water against the black sand. When he got back to Bologna he made a series of paintings.

The postcard advertising Maurizio's 'Spiaggia Nere a Mōkau' exhibition at the Galleria Polin in Treviso, March 2008.

In June 2013 we spent a week with Mimmo and Angela on the islands of Mull and Iona. For the last couple of nights we stayed in a bed and breakfast in Tobermory, just above the main street overlooking the harbour. On our last night we went to a restaurant for dinner and then to a pub on the waterfront. Mimmo did not want to walk back up the hill because he was having some trouble with his hip and knee, so we asked the barman if he would phone a taxi. He called and was told that we would have to wait for an hour. We asked if there were any other taxis in Tobermory and the barman said, 'Yes, there are two more on the island, but one is broken down and the other driver is drunk.' We settled down for another drink.

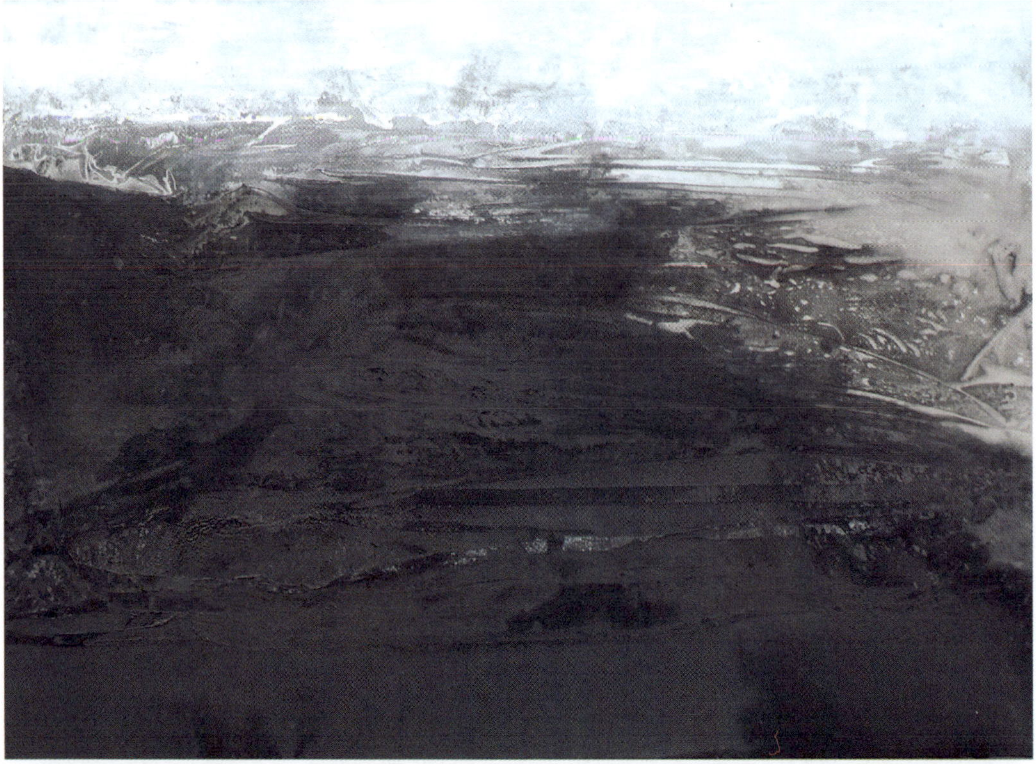

Two paintings from the 'Spiaggia Nera a Mōkau' exhibition.

Lecce Monastery.

With his soaring tenor voice Giacomo longed to become known as Il Sacredote di Canto – the singing priest. The honeyed tones of his alluring voice penetrated the thick limestone walls of Il Convento Faggiano where an impressionable novice, Mariella Aguzzo prayed and hung on every note. In the balmy summer evenings, with the delicate fragrance of olive blossoms and a glass of primitivo from the Abbey of Santa Maria di Cerrutti . . .

A casket bearing the figure of Christ, a heavy statue of Mary carried by strong men, splendid ladies in mantillas, elegant dignitaries and a sprucely uniformed band with the conductor marching backwards followed the archbishop and bishops in full regalia through the sumptuous baroque streets of Lecce in the 2009 Good Friday procession. The band played majestic funeral dirges.

Six years earlier the sound of a much smaller and less splendidly clad band warming up for the Via Crucis procession from the church of Santa Maria della Pietà in Palermo caught our ears. It comprised five or six brass instruments, two clarinets, three flutes and a bass drum. With gloriously raucous intonation they played solemn funeral marches like *Pianto Eterno* and *Lacrime e Fiori*. White sheets hung from the tenement windows as they marched through the narrow streets for five hours behind the catafalque and statue of the Virgin Mary. There was applause when the crouching bearers managed to bring Mary through the church door without knocking her head off. Every now and then during the procession purple-robed men sounded wooden clappers to signal a pause for a short rest for the band and statue bearers. Not long before we had attended a Scottish Opera performance of Wagner's *Götterdämmerung*. This band beat five hours of Wagner.

Lacrime e Fiori.

The band for the 2009 Good Friday procession in Siracusa, like that of Lecce, was bigger and smarter. The dirges were more dignified but equally impressive. On Santo Sabato or Holy Saturday we were taken in by the lovely hospitable Sicilian family of a chef, Carmelo who lived near Modica. We had met him earlier through a friend. The proceedings began with a lavish lunch followed by a search for wild asparagus and herbs in the surrounding fields. Later in the afternoon we were taken to the nearby town of Scicli for an aperitivo and gossip in the barber's shop while Carmelo was given a shave and haircut. After more exquisite food we went to the Chiesa di Santa Maria della Consolazione where, on the stroke of midnight, the statue of Christ rose up from behind the altar in clouds of incense and dry ice and the throng of people packing the church clapped, jumped up and down, shouted, laughed, made a joyful noise and shouted 'Gioia! Gioia! Gioia!', nearly bringing the building down. Then they took to the streets and had races with catafalques and statues.

An entirely different ritual in Sardinia is the ancient game of morra. Simultaneously one person throws out a hand showing a number of fingers and the other shouts out a guess at the number. If the answer is correct the shouter takes the point. When money is involved heated arguments have led to murder. Sometimes the game has been banned. We played for fun.

Easter in Greece is a time when many people return to their home village for a few days to join family and friends and, after the restraints of the forty days of Lent, devour the traditional roasted or barbecued goat. In towns all over Greece the Epitaphios procession takes place on Good Friday. In Leonidhion on the east coast of the Peloponnese, catafalques covered in flowers are carried in solemn candle-lit procession from each church to the town square for prayers and then returned. The fun comes after the resurrection service at midnight on Saturday. Bells ring, fire crackers are set off, hot-air balloons sent up and an effigy of Judas is burnt.

Easter in Leonidhion.

On Good Friday in Neochori on the west coast of the Peloponnese, we processed through all three wonderfully frescoed churches and ducked under the catafalque before going into the main church for the Lamentation of Christ with the resonant chanting of the priest. We emerged to bells, flashes of lightning, fireworks and howling dogs. When Archbishop Seraphim of Athens and All Greece died on 10 April 1998 the bells of Neochori and throughout Greece rang:

G'dong g'dong g'dong
G'dong g'dong g'dong
G'dong g'dong
G'dong g'dong
G'dong g'dong g'dong

'He dies rich and famous, with great splendour while the poor are just buried, even though we all die,' said the black-clad widows.

The sound of plainsong coming from the church in the pretty Dordogne village of Loubressac attracted our attention. We sat on the steps outside to listen, but did not go in in case we might disturb something private. The singing stopped and six men came out. They were monks from the monastery of Conques going from church to church singing plainsong. Two elegant women carrying poodles then went into the church.

Frequent travel between New Zealand and Scotland has allowed for visits to Australia, Cambodia, China, Dubai, Hong Kong, India, Indonesia, Israel, Japan, Malaysia, Philippines, Singapore, Taiwan and Thailand – sometimes for performances of my music along the way.

Mariella, with a keen ear for music, gave herself freely to tears of joy at the sound of that voice.

My father did not have a soaring tenor voice and my mother was never a novice. Any involvement with the Catholic Church would have been anathema to them.

Travelling in Cambodia.

To cut a long story short they met by chance at the Porta Napoli. Giacomo, entranced by Mariella's beauty, could not stop himself from bursting into Puccini's great love song 'Ti amo'. Mariella, captivated, swooned. He swept her up and carried her to the nearest hotel and there, it seems, I was conceived.

The suggestion that my father might have seduced my mother is wildly beyond the pale. The circumstances in which they met and courted could not, I am sure, have been described as romantic, unless my grandparents' dark dining room, or an austere and dingy church hall with a board on the wall listing all those 'promoted to glory', might be thought of as romantic.

Quickly they became the talk of the monasteries and convents of Puglia and beyond. For some it was a chink of light in war-torn Italy, but for others a monumental sin and scandal. In disgrace and with the power of the church on their tails they decided to flee the country. Finding sympathetic ears in an American bomber group stationed in Lecce, they were whisked away to begin their journey to the other side of the world.

An airstrip set up in Lecce in 1943 was used by American bombers carrying out raids in France, Romania, Czechoslovakia, Hungary, Germany and Italy, including over Bologna.

In New Zealand Giacomo and Mariella anglicised their names and became Jack Cresswell and Muriel Sharp. They forswore the demon primitivo, renounced Catholicism, joined the Salvation Army and were married in Wellington.

I was brought up in a strictly teetotal family. As an adolescent I signed the Salvation Army 'Articles of War', in which I declared that:

> I will abstain from the use of all intoxicating liquors and from the habitual use of opium, laudanum, morphia and all other baneful drugs, except when in illness such drugs shall be ordered for me by a doctor.

and . . .

> I will abstain from the use of all low or profane language.

I have to confess that I have not kept to these promises.

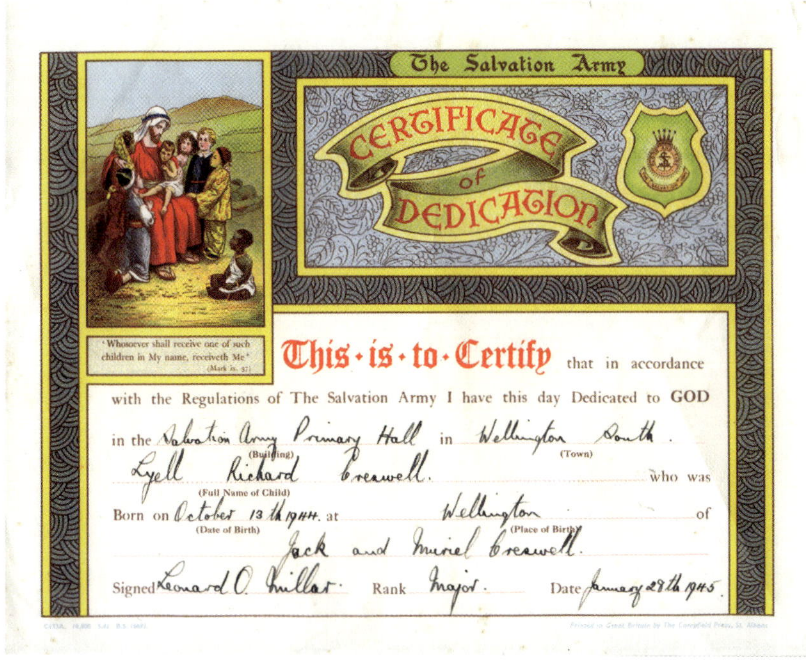

The Salvation Army

CERTIFICATE of DEDICATION

'Whosoever shall receive one of such children in My name, receiveth Me' (Mark ix. 37)

This is to Certify that in accordance with the Regulations of The Salvation Army I have this day Dedicated to GOD in the Salvation Army Primary Hall (Building) in Wellington South (Town). Lyell Richard Creswell. (Full Name of Child) who was Born on October 13th 1944. (Date of Birth) at Wellington (Place of Birth) of Jack and Muriel Creswell.

Signed Leonard O. Millar. Rank Major. Date January 28th 1945.

I was dedicated to the Salvation Army when I was four-and-a-half months old.

Mariella/Muriel gave birth to me in the Salvation Army hospital for unmarried mothers.

Mariella – star of the sea, Muriel – white sea.

Refusing to speak Italian ever again, they quickly became assimilated and learned to obliterate all trace of their mother tongue. I was brought up without a word of Italian, but with the clandestine rosary in one hand and the booming bass drum in the other.

I was indeed brought up without a word of Italian. I have since learnt one or two, some of them low and profane.

Jack and Muriel were determined to nurture me in a musical environment. Early attempts to teach me to play the mandolin failed. With the mouth organ things only improved slightly, but then I was thrown into the brass band and took to it like a duck to water.

There were no attempts to teach me to play either the mandolin or the mouth organ, and while there was music around, there was no particular encouragement to follow a musical path. Nevertheless from a very early age I was entranced by both the sight and the sound of the brass band.

My real pleasure however came from listening to the band music and writing down musical patterns.

From puerile beginnings I have gone a little way towards learning how to write down musical patterns. It will take at least another 30 years to master these skills. Three examples of my efforts have a particular connection with the work of Maurizio Bottarelli – *I paesaggi dell'anima*, *Atta* and *Ylur*.

I paesaggi dell'anima was written as part of a project with Mimmo exploring the links between music, painting and landscape. The plan was to look at the affinities between the creation of painting and music through dialogue between painter and composer based on the idea of landscape. The project was to take place at the Fondazione di San Antonino e San Colombano in Piacenza, but funding problems and changes in administration prevented it from going ahead. The music and paintings, however, survive.

Atta for solo cello was written for the opening of an extensive exhibition embracing 10 years of work by Bottarelli. The exhibition took place in the Palazzo Massari in Ferrara in October 1993. The word 'atta' is old Norse for eight – a number that has assumed particular significance for Mimmo as a result of various coincidences. It also fascinates him because it is the only number, apart from zero, formed in one continuous line with no beginning or end, so the piece is in eight contrasting movements. In each movement fragments are fitted together to make an organic unit. The first performance of *Atta* was given by Marco Boni[1] in the Palazzo Massari in October 1993.

Working with Maurizio at L'Accademia di Brera in Milan.

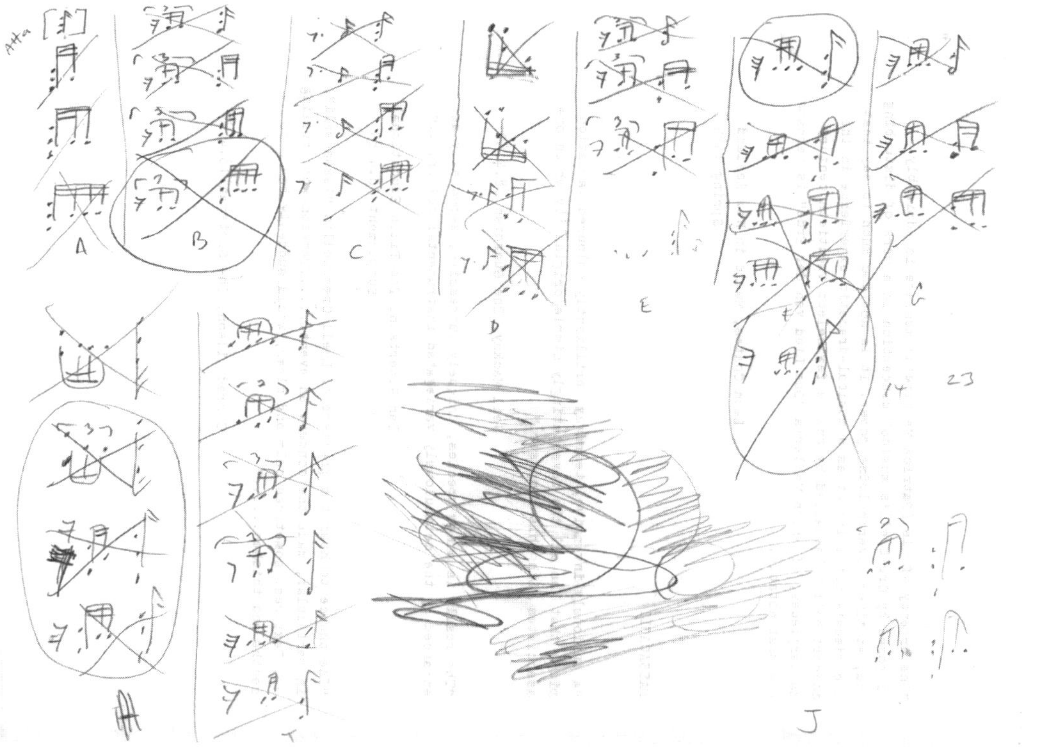

Pencil sketch for the fourth movement of Atta – *Con lancio* (vigorously).

Atta – *the opening of movement IV.*

The St Magnus Festival in Orkney commissioned a work to be played by the BBC Scottish Symphony Orchestra in 1991 along with an exhibition of related drawings by Bottarelli. During the composition of *Ylur* Mimmo came to visit and we took some time off to drive around the Scottish Highlands. Soaking up the spectacular autumnal landscape we talked about the project during the daytime and after dinner he made pastel drawings on sandpaper, working into the early hours of the morning. When he ran out of sandpaper he went to the local hardware shop to buy a packet of a hundred sheets. The shopkeeper looked at him and said, 'You must have a very big boat.'

One evening, strolling along the waterfront a grizzled, prune-like fisherman hirpled up to us and told us that the Blue Men tried to sink his boat. The Blue Men are mythological, human-like, creatures that swim in the Minch between the mainland and the Western Isles. They taunt sailors by shouting poetry and trying to lure them to their deaths in the sea.

This Bottarelli landscape, Paesaggio 2003, was used for the cover of the Wai-te-ata Music Press edition of Ylur.[2]

YLUR

♩ = 88 Risoluto
I
Lyell Cresswell.
Cor Ang.
Hn. 1
solo
pizz
Vln. I
solo
pizz
Vla.
Harmonics sound
solo at written pitch.
Cb.
Cor Ang.
Bn.
Hn.
(pizz)
Vln. I
tutti
(pizz)
Vla.
tutte (div)
Cb.
tutti (div.)

115
Picc.
Fl.
Ob.
Cor Ang.
Cl.
B. Cl.
Bn.
C. Bn.
Hn.
Tpt.
Tbn.
Perc.
Vln. I
Vln. II
Vla.
Vlc.
Cb.
Pizz
Pizz

♩ = 92 Più mosso
65
Picc.
Fl.
Ob.
Cor Ang
Cl.
B.Cl.
Bn.
C.Bn
Hn.
Tpt.
senza sord.
Tbn.
Perc.
Vln. I
Vln. II
Vla.
Vlc.
Cb.

The word 'ylur' is an old Norse expression of sorrow, sometimes heard in Orkney as 'aloor'. The music explores sorrow. As well as melancholy, grief and regret it looks at other aspects of sorrow involving anger, pain, bitterness, strength and even a delight in sorrow or, as Billie Holiday sings, 'I'm so unhappy, but oh so glad.'

Sadness is a part of any form of enjoyment; the more moving one finds any work of art the more one becomes aware of transience.

As a form of teenage rebellion I toyed with the possibility of entering the priesthood, but this was roundly discouraged.

For one brief phase of my young life I did consider training to become a Church of England priest, which my mother would have encouraged but it never became a serious option.

Only in later life did I discover that I was Giacomo's third son.

All my life I have known that I am the third son.

With my brothers Roger and Max, 1947.

Intermezzo 3
Twins

God hath given you one face, and you make yourselves another.
Shakespeare, Hamlet, *Act 3 Scene 1*

My father, Jack between his older twin brothers Frank and Ray, c.1918.

Every August student writers, musicians, actors, critics, aesthetes, dilettanti and general groupies gathered in one of the university towns for an arts festival. It was something like a small-scale Edinburgh Fringe festival, with theatrical performances, concerts, readings, films, exhibitions, happenings and parties taking place in every kind of venue. I remember the 1968 festival in Auckland very well. It was at this that I first encountered Jack Body and his music. A few years later when we met again a friendship developed.

On Saturday 7 October 1944 Jack was born in Te Aroha. Seven days later, on Friday 13 October I was born in Wellington. That year Schoenberg contemplated moving to New Zealand, but we were spared and instead the country ended up with Jack and me. Although we were born on different days and nearly 300 miles apart, we thought of each other as twins. The last thing Jack said to me in an email before he died in 2015 was, 'We are truly twins.'

Allegations against Jack of sexual harassment of students have surfaced since he died. I know nothing of the truth of these. I remember him only as a kind and loyal friend.

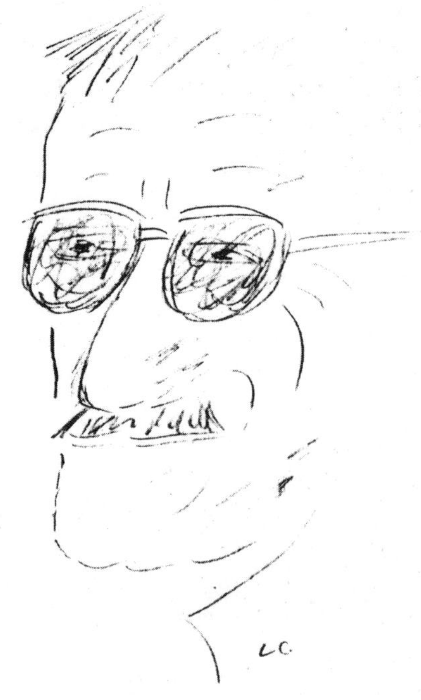

Jack in 1998.

On the retirement of Douglas Lilburn in 1980 a lectureship in composition at Victoria University was advertised. Gillian Whitehead, Jack Body and I conceived a plan to apply as a triumvirate, taking turns year about. Frederick Page (then retired), David Farquhar and the department supported the application, but it was opposed by the administration. The committee appointed to make the decision was on the point of agreeing to it when a thunderstorm struck and the meeting was adjourned. During the break the administration marshalled its forces, came up with arguments about the calculation of superannuation and the like, and the application was turned down. Divine intervention can only have caused the thunderstorm because the right decision was made.

The Edinburgh Contemporary Arts Trust (ecat) was dedicated to promoting and supporting the work of contemporary artists, especially musicians, by arranging performances and commissioning new work. In 1985 ecat commissioned me to compose a work for piano, saxophone, narrator and tape. The performers were Richard Beauchamp (piano), Dick Lee (saxophone) and Richard Irvine (narrator), and the tape was made in the studio at Glasgow University.

The work, written in collaboration with a writer, involved stories of twins. After two performances the work had to be withdrawn because parts of the text were under copyright and some of it was plagiarised from another source. I had asked the writer beforehand to check the copyright situation and he assured me that he had done so. He had not and I never worked with him again. He was a pub philosopher who enjoyed holding forth to anyone who would listen. Some years later I met him for a drink. As the drink took effect he accused me of betrayal when I told him that I was working with another writer. We parted on awkward terms and I never saw him again. On my way home, in the early hours of the morning, I passed some raucous young men. One of them called across the street to me, 'Hey, baldy old bastard!'

Some limbering up is necessary before starting any new work – always an excuse to put off starting. What the work is to be about, how it is to be done and why it needs to be done are all questions that have to be faced. To come to some understanding of the subject of twins I began to make rough sketches and became so absorbed in this that it led to a series of more than 50 drawings using mixtures of coloured ink. At the first performance in the Queens's Hall Edinburgh they were exhibited and sold. I lost track of most, but those I have been able to locate are reproduced here.

Some of the drawings that I have not been able to locate are of Ahriman and Ormuz, Baldur and Loki, Cain and Aclima, Castor and Pollux, Florus and Laurus, Helen and Clytemnestra, Hesper and Phosphor, Hun-hun-ahpu and Vukub hun-aphu, Iphikles and Heracles, Baltram and Sintram, Sieglinde and Siegmunda, Thomas and Thomas, Lucifer and Michael, Marcus and Marcellianus, Cautes and Cautopates, Monim and Aziz, Quetzalcoatl and Tezcatlipoca, Romulus and Remus, Set and Horus, Shi-acha and Mo-acha, Tathautis and Teabis, Amphion and Zethus, Kastoulus and Polyeuctes, Typhon and Osiris, and Tweedledum and Tweedledee.

And in the process of time it came to pass that Cain brought of the fruit of the ground an offering unto the Lord. And Abel, he also brought of the firstlings of his flock and of the fat thereof. And the Lord had respect unto Abel and to his offering: but unto Cain and to his offering he had not respect. And Cain was very wroth, and his countenance fell. And the Lord said unto Cain, 'Why art thou wroth? And why is thy countenance fallen? If thou doest well, shalt thou not be accepted? And if thou doest not well, sin lieth at the door . . . And Cain talked with Abel his brother: and it came to pass, when they were in the field, that Cain rose up against Abel his brother, and slew him. And the Lord said unto Cain, 'Where is Abel thy brother?' And he said, 'I know not: Am I my brother's keeper?'

Genesis 4: 3–10 (*King James Bible*)

Cain and Abel.

Another version of the story is that Cain and Abel each had a twin sister – Aclima and Jumella. Cain was supposed to marry Jumella and Abel was supposed to marry Aclima but, despite her finery, Cain thought Jumella ugly and detested her. He preferred his own twin Aclima. Abel was not happy with this so Adam suggested that they settle the matter by making a sacrifice. While God accepted Abel's, he spurned Cain's and rejected his wish to marry Aclima. Now it was Cain who was not happy and he murdered his brother in a fit of pique.

Aclima and Jumella.

And the word of the Lord came unto me, saying, Son of man, set thy face against Gog, the land of Magog, prophesy against Gog, the chief prince of Meshech and Tubal, and prophesy against him, And say, Thus saith the Lord God; Behold, I am against thee, O Gog, the chief prince of Meshech and Tubal.

Ezekiel 38: 1–3 (*King James Bible*)

And when the thousand years are expired, Satan shall be loosed out of his prison, And shall go out to deceive the nations which are in the four quarters of the earth, Gog and Magog, to gather them together to battle: the number of whom is as the sand of the sea.

Revelation 20: 7–8 (*King James Bible*)

Gog and Magog.

Crispin and Crispinian, or Crispian, were twin Christian brothers from a high-class Roman family. They set off to Soissons in France as missionaries where they worked as shoemakers to support their activities. They preached and gave help to the poor. After being tortured for their faith they were thrown in the river tied to millstones, but managed to free themselves and swim to safety, only to be caught and beheaded. Another legend tells that their bodies were thrown into the sea and washed up in Kent. Crispin and Crispinian are the patron saints of cobblers and leather workers.

Crispin and Crispian.

Protasius and Gervasius were twin sons of the Milanese martyrs Vitalis and Valeria. Because they refused to make sacrifices to the Roman gods, Protasius was beaten to death and Gervasius beheaded. In 386 St Ambrose had a vision telling him where the bodies were buried and found the bones, which then provided the relics for the Basilica di Sant'Ambrogio in Milan. St Augustine tells of witnessing a man's sight being restored when he touched the bier as the relics were brought to the basilica.

Confessions, 9, 7 (*King James Bible*)

Protasius and Gervasius are patron saints of haymakers and are invoked for the discovery of thieves.

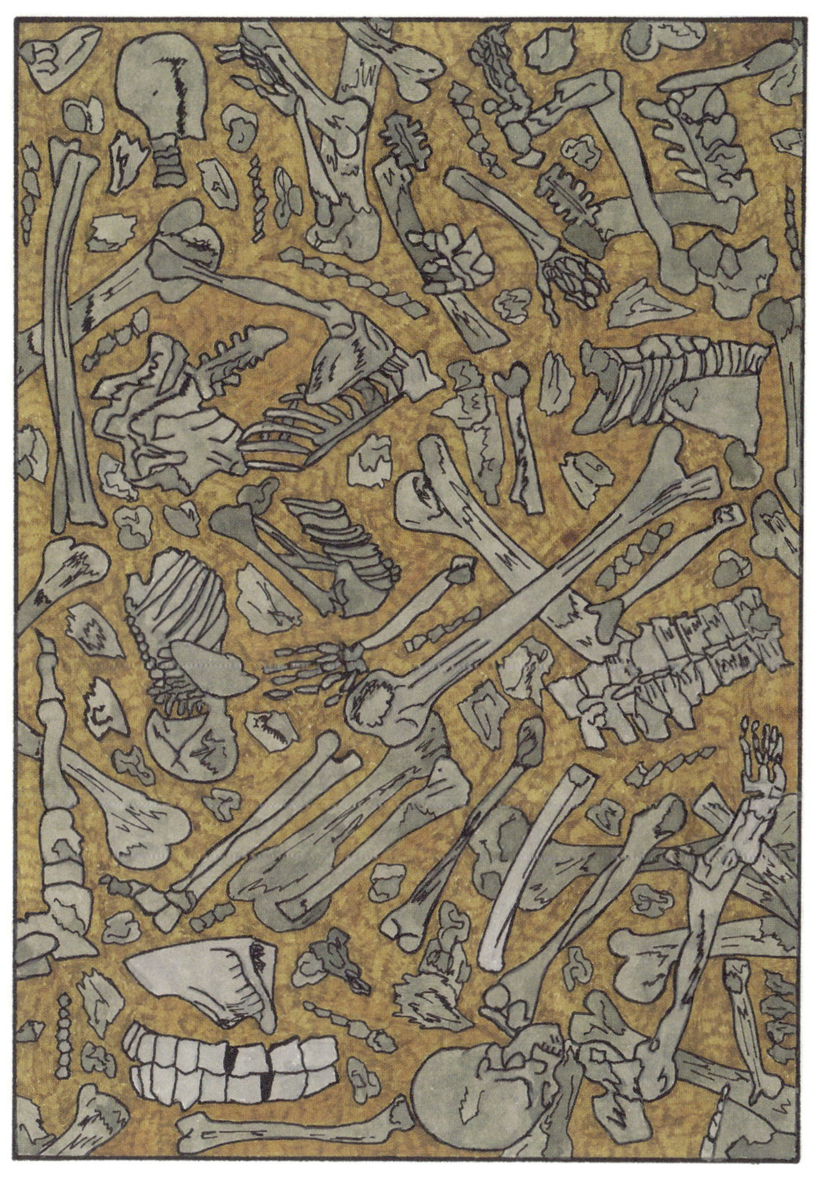

Protasius and Gervasius.

Although Taues and Taouis look rather like men in this drawing, they were twin sisters who lived in Egypt in the city of Memphis. Their mother ran off with a Greek soldier, Philippos with whom she plotted to murder her husband. Her husband escaped and fled back to his family home only to die of a broken heart. She then sold the house and turned the twins out. A recluse, Ptolemaiaeus who lived near the temple took pity on them and found them work as acolytes at the temple of the Serapeum at Saqqara representing the goddesses Isis and Nephthys, but with the connivance of their mother their stepbrother stole all their wages. The story is told in a manuscript written in Egyptian and Greek between 200 and 100 BC. It is housed in the Hermitage in St Petersburg.

Taues and Taouis.

It seems that Mutumnus and Tutumnus might have been Etruscan twin haruspices, who divined the future by scrutinising the entrails of birds. They may be confused with Turms, the Etruscan winged messenger of the gods, who took the souls of the dead to the underworld, or with Turan, the goddess of love who was associated with the white swan and the dove, or with Summamus the storm god who threw thunderbolts and lightning, or perhaps with Mutunus Tutunus, a Roman phallic god of fertility.

Mutumnus and Tutumnus.

Picumnus and Pilumnus were Roman gods of manuring the soil, pounding grain, fertility and matrimony, as well as being guardians of newborn children. The drawing is misleading because Pilumnus was either a twin brother of Picumnus or his double. Picumnus was married to Pomona, the goddess of fruit trees. However, Ovid tells in *Metamorphoses*, Book XIV that Picus (or Picumnus) married Canens and was later turned into a colourful woodpecker by Circe when he rejected her advances. Pomona was tricked into marrying Vertumnus, another agricultural god. Perhaps the drawing is really of Picumnus and Pomona, or Picus and Canens, or Picus and Circe.

Picumnus and Pilumnus.

In Brazilian mythology Tamendonaré and Arikuté were twin brothers of the Tupi people. Because of some meddlesome god they had different fathers with the result that one of the twins was a god and the other mortal. Their mother was eaten by cannibals before being able to tell them which one was the god and which one mortal. They were left wondering, and for the rest of their lives they circled round and round watching each other.

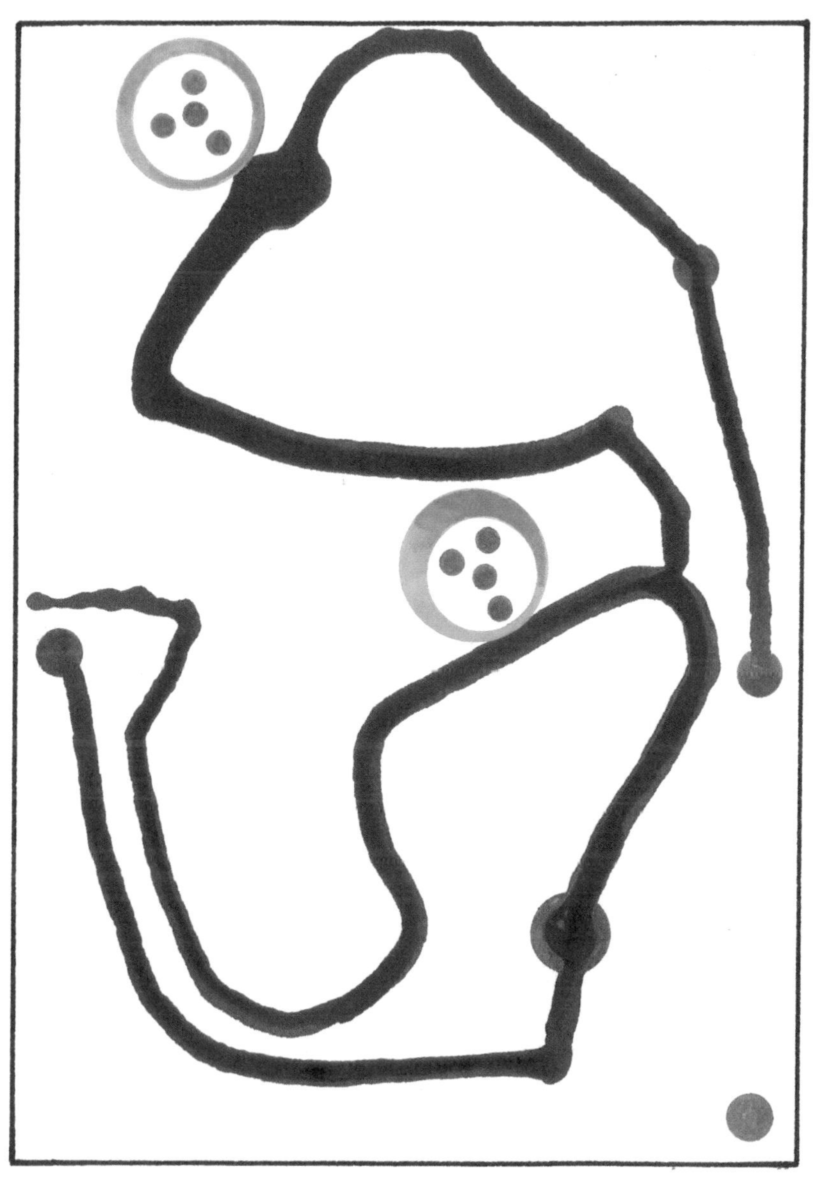

Tamendonaré and Arikuté.

Juskeha and Tawiskara were Jekyll and Hyde-like gods of the North American Huron people. Juskeha, who introduced the ritual of smoking tobacco is associated with light, goodness and life, while Tawiskara is associated with darkness, evil and death. They eyed each other with hostility and fought for dominance.

Juskeha and Tawiskara.

In Navajo mythology Tobadizini and Nayenezkani were twin sons of the sun god. They were heroes who slew malevolent gods and monsters, and meted out horrific blows to evil spirits. When they rid themselves of their first teeth they gave them to a badger. At the age of 16 they tried to find out who their father was. Begochidi, another child of the sun god – a devotee of dubious sexual practices and the inventor of pottery – told them that he was the sun god, and urged them to go and see him. Then Begochidi gave Tobadizini a ray of light and Nayenezkani a rainbow to help them on their way. They came before their father, who after many trials recognised them as his sons.

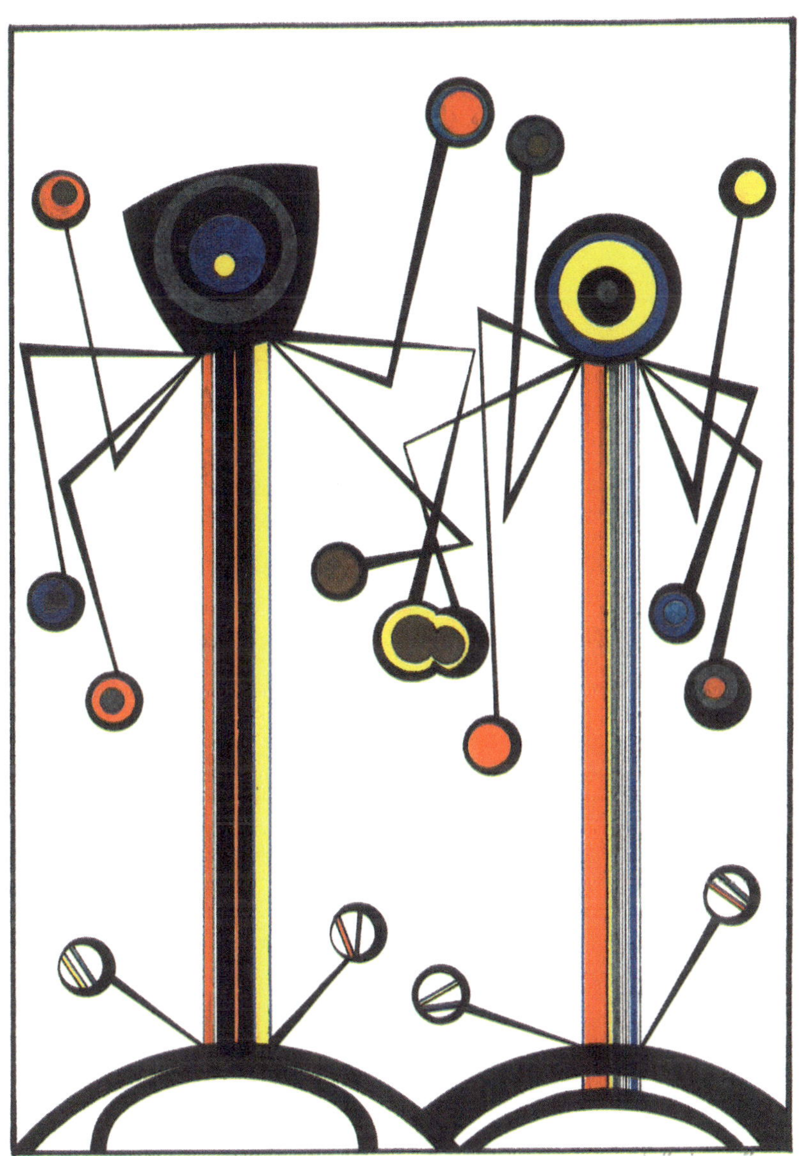

Tobadizini and Nayenezkani.

And the sons of Benjamin were Belah, and Becher, and Ashbel, Gera, and Naaman, Ehi and Rosh, Muppim, and Huppim, and Ard.
Genesis 46: 21 (*King James Bible*)

The sons of Benjamin after their families: of Bela, the family of the Belaites: of Ashbel, the family of the Ashbelites: of Ahiram, the family of the Ahiramites: of Shupham, the family of the Shuphamites: of Hupham, the family of the Huphamites.
Numbers 26: 38–39 (*King James Bible*)

Huppim and Muppim.

And it came to pass after these things, that it was told Abraham, saying, Behold, Milcah, she hath also born children unto thy brother Nahor; Huz his firstborn, and Buz his brother.

Genesis 22: 20–21 (*King James Bible*)

Rejoice and be glad, O daughter of Edom, that dwellest in the land of Uz; the cup shall pass through unto thee: thou shalt be drunken, and shalt make thyself naked.

Lamentations 4: 21 (*King James Bible*)

Huz and Buz.

Chapter 7
Friday 13 October 1944

La verità è nel fondo di un pozzo: lei guarda in un pozzo e vede il sole o la luna; ma se si butta giù non c'è più né sole né luna, c'è la verità.

Truth is in the bottom of a well: you look in a well and see the sun or the moon; but if you jump down there is no longer sun or moon, there is truth.

Leonardo Sciascia, Il Giorno della Civetta

My birth at about four o'clock in the morning on Friday 13 October 1944 was greeted with resignation – I should have been a girl. Instead, I was the third and youngest son of Jack Cecil and Muriel Minnie Cresswell, born into a family boasting generations of abstinence and religious fervour.

My great-great-grandfather, Thomas Cresswell a farm labourer from Hampshire, set sail from England on 27 April 1841 on board the *Whitby*. On 18 September, 144 days later, he disembarked at Port Nicholson on his way to Nelson. In Port Nicholson he caught typhoid and died on board ship in Nelson Haven. Thomas's first contact with the land for which he set out was his grave on Haulashore Island. His wife Amelia set sail for Nelson in September 1841. She arrived on 7 February 1842 with their three children – William (my great-grandfather), Elizabeth and Mary-Jane – unaware of Thomas's death.

My grandfather Cecil Horatio Cresswell was the third of William's seven children and an inventive man. It is said that he could pick up any musical instrument and play it immediately. Cecil married Margaret Greenaway and together they devoted their lives to the social work of the Salvation Army – caring for alcoholics and orphaned children.

My maternal grandfather Henry Proctor Sharp was an officer in the Salvation Army and not of a particularly musical bent. Some say there was not a musical bone in his body. However, it is reported that when he first saw Esther Whitehead playing the piano he said, 'I'm going to marry that woman.' It was two years before this resolution was executed. Esther (Ettie) was a talented musician. She played the violin and the piano. Her special aptitude was to pick up any tune very quickly and improvise around it on the piano. She was therefore very much embroiled in the world of Salvation Army music-making.

My parents were also involved in this world. Their halting piano playing is probably the source of my individual sense of rhythm. My mother was a passionate, trembling contralto. My father at different times played nearly all the instruments of the brass band. His sons, with varying degrees of enthusiasm, were encouraged to follow this practice and his brother, Ray Cresswell, was a prolific composer of gebrauchsmusik (useful music) for Salvation Army bands. Jack worked as an accountant in the civil service and Muriel, frustrated by the dearth of working opportunities for women, confined herself to bringing up the family on a typical post-war housing development at the west end of Karori.

So I was brought up in a brass band – captivated by the music, but awkward in the uniform. Along with the delights and discoveries of primary school and the frustrations of secondary education, my musical curiosity grew. My studies at the universities of Wellington, Toronto, Aberdeen, Utrecht and the Massachusetts Institute of Technology along with composer fellowships at Edinburgh and Glasgow universities ensured that I was incapable of anything other than the life of a composer.

My birth at about four o'clock in the morning on Friday 13 October 1944 was greeted with resignation – I should have been a girl. Instead, I was the third and youngest son of Jack Cecil and Muriel Minnie Cresswell, born into a family boasting generations of abstinence and religious fervour.

13 October 1944 was a Friday.

My great-great-grandfather, Thomas Cresswell a farm labourer from Hampshire, set sail from England on 27 April 1841 on board the Whitby. *On 18 September, 144 days later, he disembarked at Port Nicholson on his way to Nelson. In Port Nicholson he caught typhoid and died on board ship in Nelson Haven. Thomas's first contact with the land for which he set out was his grave on Haulashore Island. His wife Amelia set sail for Nelson in September 1841. She arrived on 7 February 1842 with their three children – William (my great-grandfather), Elizabeth and Mary-Jane – unaware of Thomas's death.*

My great-great-grandfather's story is true.

On the wall in the hallway we have a reproduction of a watercolour of Haulashore Island and Nelson Haven painted by Charles Heaphy in November 1841. The sky is cloudy and there is some snow on the far mountains. In the foreground there is a wooden building, six white tents and some activity on the beach. In the harbour there are three sailing ships and a number of other small boats. A rowing boat has just landed on the island bringing eight people. Thomas was buried on Aglionby Point, Haulashore Island, on 23 November 1841, so perhaps the men with the rowing boat are preparing for his burial and the puff of cannon smoke from one of the ships is a salute to him. The *Whitby*, which carried Thomas was a three-masted square rigger just like two of those in the harbour. It arrived in Nelson in November 1841.

My nephew Jeremy writes:

> The two three-mast ships are the *Whitby* and the *Will Watch*, and the two-mast ship is the *Arrow*. The *Arrow* was the supply ship and there was a supply depot on Haulashore Island, so it looks as if the long ship is unloading supplies rather than transporting a body. Also there is a wooden house built onshore which would not be built before a body was buried. However, Thomas probably died of typhoid on board the *Will Watch* (which was being used as a hospital hulk) after about two weeks in harbour. This would be enough time to build a prefabricated house. Also the far right three-mast barque seems to be flying a Fever Flag. On that evidence it's hard to be definitive one way or another. What makes me swing towards it being the funeral part is the fact it would have been one of the earliest 'events'

in colonial Nelson. Heaphy witnessed it and it is the central focus point of the watercolour. On the other hand, Heaphy's paintings were under contract for the New Zealand Company as propaganda to sell property in the colony. Would you put a funeral party in the centre of a boosting painting? Maybe you would if death was so common in the early 19th century that an image of a Christian burial was reassuring.

Charles Heaphy – Nelson Haven, November 1841.
Alexander Turnbull Library, Wellington NZ. Ref: C-025-015

Thomas set out from Hampshire with a friend, John Holdaway. Their wives and children followed three months later on the *Fifeshire* and landed in Nelson on 1 February 1842 without knowing that Thomas had died. On board ship Mary Holdaway gave birth and soon after arrival became ill and died. Thomas's wife, Amelia and her three children all survived the journey. There is a story that John Holdaway then approached Amelia and asked her if she would be his housekeeper. She replied, 'I will come as your wife, or not at all.' Although this cannot be verified I cling to the belief that it is true.

Haulashore Island, Nelson 2007.

On 27 February the *Fifeshire* set out for China, but just as the ship was leaving the harbour, the tide carried it on to Arrow Rock. It was wrecked and then broken up.

My grandfather Cecil Horatio Cresswell was the third of William's seven children and an inventive man. It is said that he could pick up any musical instrument and play it immediately. Cecil married Margaret Greenaway and together they devoted their lives to the social work of the Salvation Army – caring for alcoholics and orphaned children.

It was indeed said that he could pick up any musical instrument and play it immediately, but I was never aware of him doing so. He died in 1951. My only memory is of a very ill, but lovely old man sitting in an armchair in their house in the Auckland suburb of Ōrākei and giving me a chocolate. Each of his grandchildren inherited a carved wooden box, breadboard, small table or cabinet that he had made. My grandmother had been a school teacher. It was said that she could control a class of 100 children with the bat of an eyelid.

Wedding dress-ups in the garden of my grandparents' Auckland house with (from right) Max, my cousin Beverly, Roger, me and cousin David, c.1947.

One of their postings with the Salvation Army in about 1908 was to Rotoroa Island in the Hauraki Gulf, where they were involved in setting up a home for the treatment of alcoholics. My grandmother told us that she was rather apprehensive when she and her husband were first left alone on the island with twelve male 'inebriates' to look after. The only contact with the world beyond was a weekly supply boat. Later they were sent to run the Salvation Army Boys' Home in Temuka.

Temuka Boys' Home, c.1918.

My maternal grandfather Henry Proctor Sharp was an officer in the Salvation Army and not of a particularly musical bent. Some say there was not a musical bone in his body. However, it is reported that when he first saw Esther Whitehead playing the piano he said, 'I'm going to marry that woman.' It was two years before this resolution was executed. Esther (Ettie) was a talented musician. She played the violin and the piano. Her special aptitude was to pick up any tune very quickly and improvise around it on the piano. She was therefore very much embroiled in the world of Salvation Army music-making.

Apart from the graphic works, my music does not allow for the possibility of improvisation. It is not something that has caught my imagination. In Cardiff I was briefly involved with a cheery group of free improvisers who met in an old garage for jam sessions. They called themselves 'The 100 Ton Moon Orchestra'. Once or twice we played to a small forgiving audience, but free improvisation is never as much fun for the listener as it is for the performer. All too often I have sat through tedious, self-indulgent sessions that have outstayed their welcome. Jazz, on the other hand, with its own syntax and rules of engagement, makes for much more inventive and captivating improvisation.

My parents were also involved in this world. Their halting piano playing is probably the source of my individual sense of rhythm. My mother was a passionate, trembling contralto. My father at different times played nearly all the instruments of the brass band. His sons, with varying degrees of enthusiasm, were encouraged to follow this practice and his brother, Ray Cresswell, was a prolific composer of gebrauchsmusik (useful music) for Salvation Army bands.

From time to time my father would sit down at the piano and play. One of his favourite pieces was an arrangement of the overture *Poet and Peasant* by Franz von Suppé. Perhaps his halting playing style did contribute to my approach to rhythm. Some of this might be seen in the opening bars of *Mezzotinto* written for pianist Stephen De Pledge in 2007.

Jack worked as an accountant in the civil service and Muriel, frustrated by the dearth of working opportunities for women, confined herself to bringing up the family on a typical post-war housing development at the west end of Karori.

My father was an accountant in the Ministry of Works and then the State Hydro-electric Department.

The whole family in Auckland – Jack, me, Roger, Max and Muriel, 1949.

So I was brought up in a brass band – captivated by the music, but awkward in the uniform. Along with the delights and discoveries of primary school and the frustrations of secondary education, my musical curiosity grew. My studies at the universities of Wellington, Toronto, Aberdeen, Utrecht and the Massachusetts Institute of Technology along with composer fellowships at Edinburgh and Glasgow universities ensured that I was incapable of anything other than the life of a composer.

The Forman Fellowship in Composition at the University of Edinburgh was due to be advertised around the time I left Chapter Arts Centre in Cardiff, so I called Edward Harper, a friend in the music faculty, to see if an appointment had been made. He told me that applications had closed and a decision would be made soon, but if I acted quickly an application might be considered. As I drove up to Edinburgh for the interview I got a little chilled and lost my voice. Perhaps my croaking answers to questions endeared me to the panel because I was confronted with a row of smiling faces and appointed.

In August 1980 we rented a dingy third-floor flat with porous walls behind Meadowbank Stadium. I spent the first night there on my own and was woken at 2am by shouting just inches, it seemed, from my head. A voice barked, 'And next time I'll cut your fucking cock off.' It was a little disturbing, but despite many similar intrusions I kept my sanity by writing a wind quintet commissioned by Lontano,[1] *The Silver Pipes of Ur.*

The following August we moved to a delightful attic flat on the other side of Edinburgh. In spring blackbirds nested amongst the chives in the window box just a few feet from the kitchen sink. We crept around trying not to disturb as the mother sat doggedly on her eggs, even through an unseasonable snow storm. Her eyes followed us round the room. One day three of the fledglings hopped off the nest and flew away. The fourth was reluctant, but finally tottered over the edge and fluttered down into the garden. We warned the neighbours, but they said that their cat was old and blind, and would not trouble it.

Up in the attic I completed two works – the orchestral work *O!* and a large string quartet. The New Town Concert Society and the Faculty of Music both commissioned string quartets at the same time and I felt that the only way I could fulfill the two commissions was to write one big quartet in two related parts. At first the two parts were played separately, but when eventually they were put together the piece became unwieldy, so in 1999 I made substantial cuts and turned them into one compact quartet.

My duties at the university involved seeing the composition students, helping them with their work and getting on with my own. One of the students I taught, who went on to greater things, was James MacMillan.[2]

After two years the Forman Fellowship ended and Catherine's temporary job in the library of the National Museum of Scotland finished soon after. I decided to take the computer music course at the Massachusetts Institute of Technology in Boston. Just before leaving, the Cramb Fellowship in Composition at Glasgow University was advertised. I hurriedly put together an application. When we returned from Boston, Catherine was offered work as a peripatetic cello teacher in East Lothian and I was given the Cramb Fellowship which began in October 1982. The duties were much the same as in Edinburgh – helping composition students with their work and getting on with my own. My cello concerto was commissioned for the triennial Musica Nova festival organised by the University of Glasgow and the Scottish National Orchestra in 1984. The featured composers were Elliott Carter, Per Nørgård, John Casken and myself.

Jerzy Maksymiuk was appointed Chief Conductor of the BBC Scottish Symphony Orchestra in 1983 and toured Poland with the orchestra three times. He became a firm supporter of my music and took *The Magical Wooden Head* on tour in 1984 and *Speak for us, great sea* in 1985. Jerzy covered every score he conducted with heavy pencil lines and arcane signs in bold colours. On the 1985 tour he also took *Shaar* by Iannis Xenakis. When we met for the rehearsal Jerzy said to Xenakis, 'Look, I write more notes than you.'

The tours took place in troubled times in Poland. The Solidarity trade union was very active and on 19 October 1984 the priest Jerzy Popiełuszko, a supporter of Solidarity, was murdered by agents of the security service. Audiences at the concerts were very appreciative of the visit and in Kraków I talked to some who were moved to tears by it.

With Jerzy Maksymiuk and the BBC Scottish Symphony Orchestra, Warsaw Autumn festival, 1985. The stems of the flowers cast an unfortunate shadow.
Andrej Glanda, courtesy of POLMIC – Polskie Centrum Informacji Muzycznej

Speak for us, great sea was played in the overblown barn of the Albert Hall in the 1989 BBC Proms. The title is from the poem 'Great Sea' by Charles Brasch. The most enjoyable part of the experience was the rehearsal, where I could listen pretty much on my own in that huge space from one of the few places where the music was clear. I had the same feeling when my accordion concerto *Dragspil*, commissioned for the 1995 Proms for the virtuoso accordionist James Crabb, was played. I chose the rather inelegant title in a rash moment when it was suggested by a friend, the Icelandic composer Hafliði Hallgrímsson.

The Cramb Fellowship ended in 1985. By that time I was receiving a steady flow of commissions and with Catherine working as a peripatetic cello teacher again we were able to make ends meet. I began working as a full-time composer. We are well practised at living on a low income without the luxury of an academic salary, but we have been lucky to be able to live rich lives.

For my fiftieth birthday in 1994 some concerts were organised in Glasgow and Edinburgh by the BBC, ecat and the Chamber Group of Scotland. A large poster advertising 'Lyell Cresswell Is Fifty' and other events at the Tramway arts centre appeared in a number of places – most prominently in the Glasgow underground stations.

The chamber music concerts included various pieces of mine as well as Gillian Whitehead's song-cycle *Awa Herea* and Jenny McLeod's *Piano Piece* (1965). The first BBC concert included *A Modern Ecstasy, O!* and *Ylur,* along with *Troork*, a trombone concerto by Xenakis written for Christian Lindberg. Lindberg was impressed with what he heard and this led to the commissioning by the Scottish Chamber Orchestra of *Kāea*, my own trombone concerto, for him.

My relationship with both the Scottish Chamber Orchestra (director, Roy McEwan) and the BBC Scottish Symphony Orchestra (director, Hugh Macdonald) have been very good. The BBC Scottish Symphony Orchestra has played many of my works. For a time, whenever I was spotted entering the hall for a concert while the orchestra was warming up, one of the horn players was heard playing the first few bars of *Ylur.*

New Zealand, New Music, 1998 – the logo is my design.

ecat in collaboration with the BBC and the universities of Edinburgh and Glasgow, presented festivals of New Zealand music in Edinburgh and Glasgow in 1998 and 2001. I was the artistic director. New Zealand composers John Psathas, Helen Bowater and Ross Harris were commissioned to write works.

On the day of the climactic orchestral concert in Greyfriars Kirk there was an early snowfall, but we all managed to keep warm and catch up in convivial gatherings.

At the BBC Scottish Symphony Orchestra rehearsal in Greyfriars Kirk, Edinburgh on Saturday 5 December 1998. From left clockwise: Gordon Burt, Jack Body, John Psathas, Helen Bowater, me and Gillian Whitehead. Andrew Caldwell

John Cousins and his wife, Colleen Anstey, Catherine, me and Jack Body, Glencoe, 2001.

John Cousins, me (holding Franz Schubert)), Andrew Caldwell and Helen Bowater in the pantry, 4 Leslie Place, Edinburgh.

New Zealand, New Music

Having introduced British listeners to a distinctive and fascinating group of New Zealand composers in 1998, ECAT once more turns the spotlight on the liveliest voices from Aotearoa today.

Thursday 29 November 1.10pm FREE EVENT

Concert Hall, University of Glasgow
Funded by the Ferguson Bequest
North Atlantic/South Pacific Festival of Contemporary Music
New Zealand, New Music concerts in Glasgow are part of the North Atlantic/South Pacific Festival of Contemporary Music, presented by Music in the University, in association with ECAT, as part of the 550th anniversary of the University of Glasgow.
For details of all the concerts in this series please contact the University of Glasgow 2001 Events Hotline Tel: 0141 330 2001.

New Zealand String Quartet
with Richard Beauchamp, piano

Iain Matheson	How Long Things Last (First performance, commissioned by ECAT with subsidy from Scottish Arts Council)
John Psathas	Abhisheka
Lyell Cresswell	And Every Sparkle Shivering

Thursday 29 November 7.45pm TICKETS £9 (Concessions £4)

Greyfriars Kirk, Edinburgh *See Ticket Information*

New Zealand String Quartet
with Richard Beauchamp, piano

Iain Matheson	How Long Things Last (Commissioned by ECAT with subsidy from Scottish Arts Council)
Ross Harris	Ghost Dances
Jack Body	Three Transcriptions
John Psathas	Abhisheka
Lyell Cresswell	And Every Sparkle Shivering

Friday 30 November 7.45pm FREE TICKETS

Greyfriars Kirk, Edinburgh *See Ticket Information*

BBC Scottish Symphony Orchestra with the New Zealand String Quartet
Kenneth Young, conductor
BBC Invitation Concert to be recorded for broadcast on BBC Radio 3

Jack Body	Pulse
Ross Harris	Music for Jonny
Helen Bowater	River of Ocean (First performance, commissioned by ECAT with subsidy from Creative New Zealand)
Eve de Castro-Robinson	Other Echoes
Lyell Cresswell	Concerto for Orchestra and String Quartet

Saturday 1 December 1.10pm TICKETS £4

Greyfriars Kirk, Edinburgh *See Ticket Information*

Scottish Voices, directed by Graham Hair
with Charles Bell, narrator and Tommy Foster, percussion

Jack Body	Love Sonnets of Michelangelo
Gillian Whitehead	Movements from Nga Haerenga
Ross Harris	Sleep, O Beloved (First performance, commissioned by ECAT with subsidy from Scottish Arts Council)

Saturday 1 December 7.45pm
Presented by Scottish Chamber Orchestra

Queen's Hall, Edinburgh

Scottish Chamber Orchestra,
conducted by Joseph Swensen, includes Lyell Cresswell's The Pumpkin Massacre. Further details from SCO Tel: 0845 270 7812

Sunday 2 December 7.45pm TICKETS £9 (Concessions £4)

Reid Concert Hall, Edinburgh *See Ticket Information*
presented in association with Edinburgh University Concerts

Composer as Performer
presented by Jack Body

Alison Isadora	Country of Origin
Philip Dadson	Plate Techtonics
John Cousins	Ssaufhapt
Philip Dadson	Drum-Head
Ross Harris	Circle of Light
John Cousins	Songs for the Little Lady

Monday 3 December 7.30pm FREE EVENT

Concert Hall, University of Glasgow
Funded by the Ferguson Bequest
North Atlantic/South Pacific Festival of Contemporary Music

Glasgow University Sound Diffusion
electro-acoustic concert featuring works by visiting composer John Cousins and new work by William Sweeney

Tuesday 4 December 1.10pm FREE EVENT

Reid Concert Hall, Edinburgh
presented in association with Edinburgh University Concerts

Stephen De Pledge, piano

Ross Harris	A path to memory
John Psathas	Waiting for the aeroplane
Helen Bowater	Wire Dogs
John Rimmer	For the Kokako
Gareth Farr	Sepuluh Jari

Tuesday 4 December 5.15pm FREE EVENT

University of Edinburgh Faculty of Music
presented in association with University of Edinburgh

Composer as Performer
Seminar chaired by Jack Body, with Ross Harris, Alison Isadora, John Cousins and Philip Dadson

Wednesday 5 December FREE EVENT

St Mary's Music School, Edinburgh
presented in association with St Mary's Music School

The Transcendental Piano
Dan Poynton, piano
Workshop 2.00pm, Recital 6.00pm

John Psathas	Fragment
Jack Body	14 Stations
Annea Lockwood	Red Mesa
John Bayer	Smell o' the Boards
Dan Poynton	Nga Iwi E
Dan Poynton	The Lugubrious Troubadour

Due to space restrictions, entry to both the Workshop and Recital is by invitation. Please contact ECAT if you wish to receive an invitation.

Thursday 6 December 1.10pm FREE EVENT

Concert Hall, University of Glasgow
Funded by the Ferguson Bequest
North Atlantic/South Pacific Festival of Contemporary Music

Scottish Voices, directed by Graham Hair
with Charles Bell, narrator and Tommy Foster, percussion programme as 1 December in Edinburgh and new work by John Gormley

Sunday 9 December 7.30pm
Presented by University of Glasgow

Bute Hall, University of Glasgow
North Atlantic/South Pacific Festival of Contemporary Music

University of Glasgow Choral Society,
conducted by Christopher Bell, performs Graham Hair's The Great Circle.

Call 0141 330 2001 for tickets - £6 (Concessions £3).

Programme for New Zealand, New Music, 2001. Stephen De Pledge was unable to attend and Dan Poynton gave a recital instead.

Only a small part of my mature work has been composed in New Zealand. In July 2006 I took up the year-long Creative New Zealand/New Zealand School of Music Composer Residency. This gave me the chance to alter this balance and for the first time I was able to work in my country on some large-scale orchestral music. It was a fruitful and enjoyable year. We lived in the splendidly situated modernist house at 22 Ascot Street where Douglas Lilburn lived from 1959 until his death in 2001. The house was designed by Frederich Schwarzkopf, who with his wife came to New Zealand as refugees from the Nazi occupation of Austria in 1940. The torment from their wartime experiences led eventually to their joint suicide in 1961. The property is now maintained and administered by the Lilburn Residence Trust.

Checking for mail at the Lilburn House in Thorndon, Wellington. Alan Knowles

Our predecessor in the house was Gillian Whitehead. Throughout the year Gillian was a constant and very welcome guest. The handover period for the residency seemed to last all year. One night after dinner and some glasses of wine we sat talking. Gillian seemed to be falling asleep and quite suddenly looked up and uttered these profound words, 'retrieving the fragility of the voice'.[3]

Gillian, Jack Body, me and Jenny McLeod celebrating Gillian's official farewell from the Lilburn House, July 2006. Lilburn Residence Trust

During the course of the year I completed a number of small-scale works and two larger orchestral ones – *Alas! How Swift* for trumpet and orchestra commissioned by the NZSO, and *Canterbury Rhymes* – settings of poetry by Fiona Farrell and Mary Ursula Bethell for mezzo-soprano and orchestra, commissioned by the Christchurch Symphony Trust.

2010 was an important year for me. For about 15 years I had in mind the idea of writing a piano concerto. The opportunity arose when Stephen De Pledge urged me to write one for him and thanks to the support of Jack Richards[4] we were able to carry this through.

For a long time I felt uncomfortable writing for the piano – what to do with all those fingers? Now I am fascinated by the lyrical and percussive sound world the instrument offers. Always when I am writing for it I make sure that, one way or another, I can get my fingers around all the notes I have written. In the 1990s I began a series of pieces for solo piano with titles related either to specific paintings or to painting techniques. The first of these pieces, *Who's Afraid of Red, Yellow and Blue*, takes its name from paintings by Barnett Newman. There is no background only the bright foreground music of primary colours divided up by loud percussive chords. The others are *Acquerello* (watercolour), which revolves around two quiet and contrasting ideas – one slow, one fast, *Mezzotinto* (half-tint), which investigates the softer gradations of tone between black and white, *Chiaroscuro*, which makes a simple contrast between light and shadow, *Impasto*, exploring thickly applied paint, and *White Relief*. In the 1930s Ben Nicholson produced a series of white paintings made by sticking layers of board on to one another or by carving into the surface. He likened the pure formal relationships in these paintings to musical harmonies. These six make up a set of pieces that may be played separately or together.

The concerto for Stephen De Pledge was written in memory of a close friend, the English composer Edward Harper. Edward worked for many years at Edinburgh University. He died on Easter Sunday in 2009 from a cancer that he had been fighting for four years. The concerto is in seven short movements, four of which were written before he died and the others afterwards.

When we came from New Zealand to Scotland in 1972 we left family and friends behind to see where life would take us. Questions inevitably arose. What is it like not to live in the country of your birth? What is it like not to live within reach of the shelter of family and compatriots? And what is it like not to know where you belong? We still face these questions, but a European whānau has developed around us, which has embraced us and enriched our lives. Heather and Jamie Fleck, old friends from Aberdeen, are important members of this whānau and one of the central members of it was Edward Harper. He also had a New Zealand connection. His paternal grandmother was born in Dunedin. She was the daughter of a sea captain who took his wife to New Zealand only to abandon her there, take off to sea and never be heard of again. Mother and daughter returned to England soon after his disappearance. Edward's maternal grandmother, on the other hand, was a lady of some refinement and caused some consternation in the family when she ran off with the local blacksmith. The only place where they could carry out their courtship was at the bandstand during recitals by the village band.

Edward and Louise Harper at Eggendorf near Vienna, October 2004.

The second piano concerto was commissioned by and written for Michael Houstoun. The first performance was given by the Auckland Philharmonia conducted by Johannes Fritzsch in October 2017. It is based on six chorales harmonised by J.S. Bach, none of which were written by Bach himself. The German Protestant tradition of singing hymns in the vernacular grew from a variety of styles, ranging from medieval plainsong to folk song and the song of the Meistersinger. They were originally intended to replace parts of the mass or to complement it. The congregation could therefore take a much greater and more meaningful part in the various rites.

The pre-concert talk with Eve de Castro-Robinson on 19 October 2017 – minutes after the announcement that the new Prime Minister would be Jacinda Ardern.
Studio Guidon

In essence the concerto is a set of variations, but instead of using just one theme there are six. Although different in character they are intrinsically related to one another. They guide the listener through the various twists and turns of the music. The use of the chorales provided a technical challenge – how to move freely and convincingly between clear and indistinct tonality.

Some jottings for the concerto.

The six chorales were chosen for their texts, which speak of doubts, fears, defiance, hope, joy, resignation, agony, sadness, futility and so on – perhaps bringing to mind the opening of the book of Ecclesiastes: 'Vanity of vanities, saith the Preacher, vanity of vanities; all is vanity.'

Trotz des Todes Rachen,
Trotz der Furcht darzu!
Tobe, Welt, und springe,
Ich steh hier und singe
In gar sichrer Ruh.
Gottes Macht hält mich in acht;
Erd und Abgrund muss verstummen,
Ob sie noch so brummen.
Johann Franck (1618–77)

In spite of the jaws of death,
In spite of fear of them
Rage, world, and leap,
I stand here and sing
In utterly secure peace.
God's might takes care of me;
Earth and abyss must keep silent,
Even though they grumble on.

O Traurigkeit,
O Herzeleid!
Ist das nicht zu beklagen?
Gott des Vaters einig Kind
Wird ins Grab getragen.
Freidrich Spee von Langenfeld (1591–1635)

O sadness,
O heartache!
Is that not something to complain about?
God the Father's only child
Is carried to the grave.

O Ewigkeit, du Donnerwort,
O Schwert, das durch die Seele bohrt,
O Anfang sonder Ende!
O Ewigkeit, Zeit ohne Zeit,
Ich weiß für großer Traurigkeit
Nicht, wo ich mich hinwende!
Mein ganz erschrocknes Herz erbebt,
Daß mir die Zung am Gaumen klebt.
Johann Rist (1607–67)

O eternity, you thunderous word,
O sword, that pierces the soul,
O beginning without end!
O eternity, time without time,
From such great sadness
I don't know where to turn!
My terrified heart shakes,
So that my tongue sticks to the roof of my mouth.

Ach wie flüchtig, ach wie nichtig
Ist der Menschen Leben!
Wie ein Nebel bald entstehet
Und auch wieder bald vergehet,
So ist unser Leben, sehet!
Melchior Franck (1580–1639)

Ah, how fleeting, ah how futile
Is the life of man!
As a mist soon arises
And then soon passes,
Behold! so is our life.

Ich hab mein Sach Gott heimgestellt,
er mach's mit mir, wie's ihm gefällt,
soll ich allhier noch länger leb'n,
nicht widerstreb'n,
seim Willen tu ich mich ergeb'n.
Johann Leon (1530–97)

I have left all my affairs up to God,
Let Him do with me as he pleases
Should I live here any longer,
I will not resist,
I will yield to his will.

Ihr Gestirn, ihr hohen Lüfte
und du lichtes Firmament,
tiefes Rund, ihr dunklen Klüfte,
die der Widerschall zertrennt,
jauchzet fröhlich, lasst das Singen
jetzt bis durch die Wolken dringen.
Johann Franck (1618–77)

Ye stars, ye high winds
and you bright firmament
deep round, ye dark chasms,
that the echo distorted,
shout joyfully, let the singing
penetrate through the clouds.

Early in 2020 I wrote to Stephen De Pledge to say I was thinking of a third piano concerto. His response in an email was:

> A piano concerto! I would be so overjoyed. The no.1 was quite simply one of my favourite musical experiences ever. I'd be there with bells and whistles on! Presumably there would be bells and whistles??

The various moods and feelings aroused by the extraordinary circumstances of Covid-19 and the lockdown of 2020 are reflected in the third piano concerto. I began work on it that year in the beautiful surroundings of Whatamango Bay in the Marlborough Sounds and completed it in Edinburgh in September 2021.

A great delight visiting Christchurch is sitting alone in a black leather armchair, in a small and dark space, surrounded by black curtains. One might feel a little uneasy in such surroundings, but the reassuring voice of John Cousins coming from all angles quickly dispels any anxiety, and inveigles one into a deep, moving and magical acousmatic world. John describes it as:

> . . . a place where I habitually create an imaginative universe where my sensations are amplified within an interactive environment. Here I can be alone with my thoughts and feelings, safe in a resonant, dark, warm space where my preferences hold complete sway. A place where I am able to reassure myself of my own worth, and render extant objects from that conviction. Where no other individual can impose their point of view. I am sure this is the reason why I have never been a successful collaborator, or responder to outside commissions. There can be no 'faking' here. Direct, honest, real emotions and responses are imperative.[5]

With John Cousins in Christchurch, March 2007.

Umberto Eco puts this another way when he writes:

> . . . in this world you either read or write, and writers write out of contempt for their colleagues, out of a desire to have something good to read once in a while.[6]

After the orchestral concert at the end of the 1998 New Zealand, New Music festival there was a reception in the Edinburgh City Chambers with the obligatory short speeches. A splendidly red-coated usher introduced Hugh Macdonald as 'the director of the BBC Scottish Sympathy Orchestra'. Perhaps one of the horn players in the orchestra foreshadowed this remark after a rehearsal a few years earlier when he came up to me and said, 'Mr Cresswell, you're a hooligan.'

Coda

There was things which he stretched, but mainly he told the truth.
Mark Twain, The Adventures of Huckleberry Finn

In 2016 I received an Arts Foundation Laureate Award. In my brief acceptance speech I said:

> All I have been doing over the years is writing my own biography. If I were a writer and used words instead of music I would simply have told a pack of lies, but I find it impossible to tell lies when I'm writing music. I tell my story and give my view of the world. This award makes me very happy because it tells me that, from time to time, my story strikes a chord with others – and that is all I ask.

Perhaps these pages will shed some light on the music I write.

Not long after the turn of the century a rather serious journalist interviewed me for an article he was writing about me. As we parted I gave him a copy of the 2000 Massey University Composer Address, *Tracing the Lightning Flashes*, which began with the alternative biographies of chapters 1, 2, 4 and 7. The resulting article was sympathetic, but he wrote about my 'troubled background' – how my father had been in prison, how I had overcome the difficulties of a deprived and fractured home life as a child, how my father sang sentimental songs when my mother was absent, how I had had a brush with drug-trafficking, and how eventually I had found consolation in music and channelled all these setbacks and frustrations into making something positive by writing music.

Out of the mud and sludge some disarticulated bones, cave drawings, pieces of broken glass, crockery and petrified excrement have been uncovered. Many crucial findings have yet to be revealed, and more maps and notes must be compiled.

Piero Casadei

Poem for Lyell

We met around the time the Berlin Wall was pulled apart
by ordinary men and women, just like us.
Such hope there was back then, such trust in healing.

Your music caught the world's beat, or rather
the world at last caught up with you!
Your music gave us promises not threats, humour not hatred,
harmony not division.

Sometimes I was lucky enough to work with you.
You'd stride up from Stockbridge, I'd stroll down the Southside.
Our table at the Yocoko Noodle Bar was for operas and prawns, song cycles,
a concerto, squid and duck chow mein. Green tea, wine, collaboration, friendship.

At yours, at ours, with Catherine and Regi – slow-cooked New Zealand lamb,
rösti und wurst. And always your grin and giggle,
your peering as you stooped to pour another glass all round.
Your conviviality and kindness.

Then your emails to help me get my words right:
'Too many consonants! More vowels! More vowels!' 'Can you give me
three lines of deep despair and a rollicking drunken song by Friday?'

Thirty years on and, with mostly psychopaths and clowns in charge,
the world needs your music more than ever.
And we, your friends and family, still need you. We always will.

On every side, the future stares us down.

But we can hope that we might glimpse you,
sometimes hear your voice, your laughter.
Our sadness will return, and more and more we'll know
the consolation of having found you once again.

Ron Butlin

List of Works

Most of my published and unpublished works can be bought or hired from SOUNZ Centre for New Zealand Music or the Scottish Music Information Centre. Both organisations also offer commercial and archival recordings of many of my works, as well as some video performances on YouTube.

Orchestra

Instruments are listed in the order they appear in the score:

- woodwind – flutes/oboe/clarinet/bassoon
- brass – horn/trumpet/trombone/tuba

Only the number of each of the instruments is shown. For example, '2222' means 2 flutes, 2 oboes, 2 clarinets and 2 bassoons.

Concerto for Violin and Orchestra (1970) 12'00"
Solo violin/3333/4331/timp/4perc/strings

Salm (1977) 21'00"
3333/4331/timp/3perc/harp/strings
Winner of Ian Whyte Award in 1978
Rec: Continuum CCD 1034
Pub: Wai-te-ata Music Press

The Magical Wooden Head (1980) 16'00"
0000/4331/timp/2perc/strings
Winner of Dunedin Civic Orchestra Prize in 1980

O! (1982) 16'00"
3333/4331/timp/3perc/piano/harp/strings
Commissioned by Gisborne Community Arts Council, New Zealand
Rec: Continuum CCD 1034
Pub: Wai-te-ata Music Press

Concerto for Cello and Orchestra (1984) 27'00"
Solo cello/3333/4331/timp/3perc/harp/strings
Commissioned by the Scottish National Orchestra
Rec: Continuum CCD 1033
Pub: Wai-te-ata Music Press

Speak for us, great sea (1985) 18'00"
2222/4231/timp/1perc/strings
Commissioned by the BBC
Rec: Continuum CCD 1034

A Modern Ecstasy (1986) 45'00"
Mezzo-soprano, baritone/2222/4331/timp/2perc/strings
Commissioned anonymously for the BBC Scottish Symphony Orchestra
Text: Patrick Maguire
Rec: Continuum CCD 1033

Ixion (1989) 11'00"
4444/6331/timp/perc/strings
Commissioned by the National Association of Youth Orchestras

Voices of Ocean Winds (1989) 38'00"
SSAATTBB/3333/4331/timp/3perc/harp/strings
Commissioned by Radio New Zealand
Text: Charles Brasch

Ylur (1990–91) 30'00"
2222/4330/3perc/strings
Commissioned by the St Magnus Festival
Pub: Wai-te-ata Music Press

Dragspil (concerto for accordion and orchestra) (1994–95) 29'00"
Solo accordion/2222/4331/3perc/harp/strings
Commissioned by the BBC for the 1995 Proms

Concerto for Orchestra and String Quartet (1996) 30'00"
String quartet/3333/4331/timp/3perc/harp/strings
Commissioned by the City of Aberdeen
Rec: NAXOS 8.573199

Dancing on a Volcano (1996) 12'30"
3333/4331/timp/3perc/piano/harp/strings
Commissioned by the New Zealand Symphony Orchestra
Rec: Morrison Music Trust MMT2037

Kāea (trombone concerto) (1997) 18'00"
Solo trombone/picc/fl/ob/ca/cl/bcl/bn/cbn/2hn/2tpt/strings
Commissioned by the Scottish Chamber Orchestra
Rec: Naxos 8.570824

Pianto – In memory of Roger Cresswell (1997) 6'30"
Horn/strings

The Voice Inside (concerto for violin, soprano and orchestra) (2001) 28'00"
Solo violin/soprano/2222/3211/1perc(temple blocks)/strings
Commissioned by the BBC
Text: Ron Butlin
Rec: Naxos 8.570824

Of Smoke and Bickering Flame (concerto for chamber orchestra) (2001–02) 30'00"
2222/2hn/2tpt/strings
Commissioned by the Scottish Chamber Orchestra

Shadows Without Sun (2002–03) 45'00"
Fl/picc(+a.fl)/ob/ca/cl/bcl/bn/bn(+cbn)/2hn/2tpt/tbn/piano/strings, mezzo-soprano, narrator, recording
Written for the Scottish Chamber Orchestra with a Scottish Arts Council Creative Scotland Award
Text: Ron Butlin, and Euripides translated by Don Taylor

Cassandra's Songs (2002-03) 13'30"
Mezzo-soprano/picc(+a.fl)/ob/ca/cl/bcl/bn/bn(+cbn)/2hn/2tpt/tbn/strings
Written for the Scottish Chamber Orchestra with a Scottish Arts Council Creative Scotland Award
Extracted from *Shadows Without Sun*
Texts: Ron Butlin, and Euripides translated by Don Taylor
Rec: Naxos 8.570824

The Rev. Norman McLeod's Dance (2003) 6'00"
Fl/picc/ob/ca/cl/bcl/bn/bn(+cbn)/2hn/2tpt/tbn/strings
Extracted from *Shadows Without Sun*
Scottish Arts Council Creative Scotland Award

Ara Kōpikopiko (2004) 22'00"
3333/4331/strings
Written for the BBC Symphony Orchestra following the award of the inaugural Elgar Bursary

Alas! How Swift (2006) 10'30"
Solo trumpet/2fl/ob/ca/cl/bcl/2bn/2hn/strings
Commissioned by the New Zealand Symphony Orchestra
Rec: Naxos 8.570824

Canterbury Rhymes (2006) 35'00"
Mezzo-soprano/2222/4331/3perc/harp/strings
Commissioned by the Christchurch Symphony Trust
Settings of poems by Fiona Farrell and Mary Ursula Bethell

I paesaggi dell'anima (2008) 17'00"
String orchestra (66442)
Rec: Naxos 8.573199

Concerto No. 1 for Piano and Orchestra (2009–10) 30'00"
Solo piano/3333/4331/timp/3perc/harp/strings
Commissioned by Jack Richards
In memory of Edward Harper
2011 SOUNZ Contemporary Award
Rec: Naxos 8.573199
Video: SOUNZ YouTube channel

Triple Concerto (2012) 26'00"
Solo violin, cello and piano/fl/fl(+picc)/ob/ca/cl/cl(+bcl)/2bn/2hn/2tpt/strings
Commissioned by the Scottish Chamber Orchestra and the Association Les Amis du Schweizer Klaviertrio

The Clock Stops (2013) 40'00"
Baritone /3333/4331/3perc/harp/timp/strings
Commissioned by the New Zealand Symphony Orchestra
Text: Fiona Farrell

Llanto – Clarinet Concerto (2015–16) 17'30"
Solo clarinet/picc/fl/2bn/2hn/2tpt/tbn/1perc/strings
Commissioned by the Scottish Chamber Orchestra

Concerto No. 2 for Piano and Orchestra – Ach wie flüchtig, ach wie nichtig (2016–17) 40'00"
Solo piano/3333/4331/timp/2perc/strings
Commissioned by Michael Houstoun
Video: SOUNZ YouTube Channel

Concerto No. 3 for Piano and Orchestra – (2020–22) 24'00"
Solo piano/picc/fl/ca/2cl/bcl/2tpt/4331/1perc/strings

Brass Band

Major Ricketts (1991) 4'00"
Commissioned by the BBC

Large Chamber Ensembles

Threnody for Mrs S – who was drowned at her Baptism (c.1971 or 72) 15'00"
Fl/ob/ca/cl/bcl/bn/hn/tpt/tbn/xylo/harp/narrator

Octaves of Radiation (1979) 21'00"
Fl(+picc)/ob/ca/e♭ cl/bcl/alto sax/bn/cbn
Commissioned by Harry Spaarnay

Le Sucre du Printemps (1982) 13'00"
6 bass clarinets/3 contra-bass clarinets
Commissioned by Harry Sparnaay

The Pumpkin Massacre (1987) 10'30"
7vln/2vla/2vlc/cb
Commissioned by the New Zealand Chamber Orchestra
Rec: Wai-te-ata WTA002; Sound Barrier NZ Geographic/SOUNZ
Pub: Wai-te-ata Music Press

Passacagli (1988) 17'30"
Picc/ob/ca/cl/bcl/bn/cbn/2hn/2vln/vla/vlc/cb
Commissioned by Paragon Ensemble
Rec: Continuum CCD 1031

Sextet (1988) 20'00"
2tpt/hn/2tbn/tba
Commissioned by the Open University
Rec: Metier MSV CD92014

Il Suono di Enormi Distanze (1992–93) 25'00"
Mezzo-soprano/fl(+picc)/ob(+ca)/cl/bcl/bn(+cbn)/hn/tbn/1perc/harp/2vln/vla/vlc/cb
Commissioned by the Royal Scottish Academy of Music and Drama
Text: Marco Bucchieri

The Pot of Basil (1993) 20'00"
SATB(soli)/2vln/2vla/2vlc
Commissioned by the John Currie Singers
Text: composer, after Boccaccio

Fogli Rugginosi (2000) 10'00"
Wind quintet, cello, bass
Commissioned by the University of Bologna

Con Fuoco (2004) 9'00"
Fl/ob/cl/bcl/hn/tpt/tbn/2vln/vla/vlc/cb
Commissioned by Stroma

Chamber Ensembles 2–5 players

Trio (1967) 6'00"
Clarinet, violin, piano

Opuscule (1977) 6'30"
Double bass, woodblock

Waiata Tangi (1979) 10'00"
Trumpet, violin, double bass
Commissioned by Lysis
Video: SOUNZ YouTube Channel

Soliloquy on a lambent tailpiece (1980) 10'00"
Clarinet, violin, double bass
Commissioned by Lysis
Rec: Tall Poppies TP039

Ritornelli (c.1980) 12'00"
Clarinet and trumpet
Video: SOUNZ YouTube Channel

The Silver Pipes of Ur (1981) 16'00"
Wind quintet
Commissioned by Lontano

String Quartet (revised version) (1981/99) 20'00"
Originally commissioned by the New Town Concert Society and Edinburgh University
Rec: Delphian DCD34199

Variations on a Theme by Charles Ives (1987) 14'00"
Flute, cello
Commissioned by ecat
Rec: NMC D077; SOUNZ YouTube Channel
Pub: Wai-te-ata Music Press

Hammers, Levers and Strings (1990) 10'00"
2 pianos – 4 players

Canzone (1992) 14'00"
Trombone, organ
Commissioned by John Kenny
Pub: Warwick Music Publishing

Triptych (1993) 9'00"
Clarinet, piano
Commissioned by Gisborne District Council

Of Whirlwind Underground (1999) 17'30"
E♭ clarinet, bass clarinet, bass trombone, cello, double bass
Commissioned by 175 East
Rec: Wai-te-ata WTA 008
Pub: Wai-te-ata Music Press
Video: SOUNZ YouTube Channel

And Every Sparkle Shivering (1999) 21'00"
Piano quintet
Commissioned by Chamber Music New Zealand
Rec: Wai-te-ata WTA 011
Pub: Wai-te-ata Music Press

Moto Perpetuo (2005) 6'00"
Violin, cello, piano
Commissioned by NZTrio

Even on Marimba and Guitar (2010) 4'15"
Marimba, guitar

Kōtetetete (2011) 20'00", 2016 Version – 17'30"
String quartet
Commissioned by Chamber Music New Zealand
Rec: Delphian DCD34199 (first movement)

Capricci (2014) 20'00"
String quartet
Commissioned by Dr Ian McKee
Rec: Delphian DCD34199

Ricercari (2016) 15'20"
Violin, cello
Commissioned by Glasgow University
Rec: Delphian DCD34199

Die Zaubertuba (2016) 5'00"
Four tubas

Omnigaddrum (2019) 17'00"
String quartet
Commissioned by Jamie Fleck and family

Rima (2019) 18'30"
Clarinet, string quartet
Commissioned by Maximiliano Martín

Solo Works

Variations (1978) 8'00"
Violin

Hocket (1979) 7'00"
Bass clarinet and tape delay system
Commissioned by Harry Sparnaay

Toccata (1978) 3'00"
Piano

The Urim and the Thummim (1986) 10'00"
Organ
Commissioned by Michael Bonaventure
Rec: Delphian DCD34013

Ricercare (1990) 10'00"
Organ
Commissioned by Dunblane Cathedral

Atta (1993) 21'00"
Cello
Rec: NMC D077; CD Manu 1543

The Blackness of Darkness (1993) 6'00"
Organ
Commissioned by the New Zealand Festival of the Arts
Video: SOUNZ YouTube Channel

Who's Afraid of Red, Yellow and Blue (1993) 4'00"
Piano
Rec: Rattle Rat-D074
Pub: Wai-te-ata Music Press

Bisbigliando (1993) 6'00"
Harpsichord
Commissioned by Annelie de Man

Lento (1994) 2'30"
Violin
Rec: First Hand Records FHR139

Whira (1996) 19'30"
Violin
Rec: NMC D077
Pub: Promethean Editions
Video: SOUNZ YouTube Channel

Acquerello (1998) 5'00"
Piano
Rec: NMC D077; Rattle Rat-D074

Anake (1998) 13'30"
Flute
Rec: NMC D077

Apteryx (2000) 1'30"
Piano
Commissioned by the Associated Board of the Royal Schools of Music
Rec: Metier Met CD 1053; Rattle Rat-D074
Pub: Associated Board of the Royal Schools of Music in *Spectrum 3*

The Leith at Stockbridge (2003) 0'50"
Piano
Commissioned by the Associated Board of the Royal Schools of Music
Rec: Usk 1227CDD
Pub: Associated Board of the Royal Schools of Music in *Spectrum 4*

Chiaroscuro (2005) 6'00"
Piano
Commissioned by Stephen De Pledge
Rec: Rattle Rat-D046; Rattle Rat-D074
Pub: Score Publishers
Video: SOUNZ YouTube Channel

Mezzotinto (2007) 3'40"
Piano
Rec: Rattle Rat-D074

Gathering Music (2008) 4'20"
Highland bagpipes
Commissioned by the University of Edinburgh Management School

Impasto (1985/2008) 4'20"
Piano
Rec: Rattle Rat-D074

White Relief (1987/2008) 3'00"
Piano
Rec: Rattle Rat-D074

Chatoyance (2018) 5'00"
Violin
Commissioned by the Michael Hill International Violin Competition
Video: SOUNZ YouTube Channel

Seven Little Piano Pieces (2018) 10'00"
Written for significant birthdays: *EK* (Elizabeth Kerr), *FF* (Fiona Farrell), *HA* (Helen Ainsworth), *LC* (Leon Coates), *Looby Loo* (Hazel Sheppard), *Piglets* (for . . .), *WD* (William Dart)
Video: SOUNZ YouTube Channel

The Art of Black and White 26'00"
Six piano works: *Acquerello, Who's afraid of Red, Yellow and Blue, White Relief, Impasto, Mezzotinto, Chiaroscuro*
Rec: Rattle Rat-D074

Voices and choir

Four Sentimental Songs (1971) 6'00"
Soprano, piano, bamboo chimes, bag of wooden clothes pegs
Texts: Lyell Cresswell
Rec: Rattle Rat-D074

The Slaughter of the Innocents (1977) 20'00"
School orchestra and choir
Commissioned by St. Columba's High School, Clydebank
Texts: Lyell Cresswell

Prayer for the Cure of a Sprained Back (1979) 7'00"
Mezzo-soprano
Text: translation from the Māori by Arthur S. Thomson
Rec: Metier MSV CD92014

Seven Shaker Songs (1980) 15'00"
Baritone, piano
Texts: anonymous 19th century Shaker texts

O Let the Fire Burn (1981) 20'00"
SATB a cappella
Commissioned by the Bach Choir of Wellington
Texts: anonymous 19th century Shaker texts
Pub: Wai-te-ata Music Press

Eight Shaker Songs (1985) 15'00"
Soprano, piano
Texts: anonymous 19th century Shaker texts

To Aspro Pano Sto Aspro (White on White) (1986) 21'00"
SATB (divisi) a cappella
Commissioned by Cappella Nova
Texts: Yannis Ritsos
Rec: Linn CKD 014

Six Poems by Amy Lowell (1986) 6'00"
Soprano, piano
Pub: Wai-te-ata Music Press

Words for Music (1989) 4'00"
Mezzo-soprano
Commissioned by the New Zealand High Commission, London
Text: C. K. Stead
Rec: Metier MSV CD92014; BMS 420/421CD

Tre Canti (1993–94) 6'00"
Soprano, piano
Texts: Marco Bucchieri
Rec: Rattle Rat-D074

Snatches, from Baptized Generations (1993–94) 15'00"
Tenor, piano
Commissioned by Aberdeen University
Texts: Emily Dickinson
Rec: Rattle Rat-D074

Prayer to Appease the Spirit of the Land (1996) 2'00"
Soprano, recorder
Commissioned by John Turner
Text: translation from the Māori by Arthur S. Thomson
Rec: Metier MSV CD92036

The Heavenly Aeroplane (1999) 4'30"
Soprano, clarinet, violin, viola, cello
Commissioned by Irene Drummond
Text: anon, gospel song

A Recipe for Whisky (2008) 3'00"
Baritone, temple blocks
Commissioned by NMC
Text: Ron Butlin
Rec: NMC D150

Pater Columba (2010) 7'00"–10'00"
SATB a capella, or SATB and wind septet – various versions and combinations of instruments
Commissioned by the Inchcolm New Music Ensemble of Heriot-Watt University
Texts from the *Inchcolm Antiphoner*

The Harp Sang (2011) 5'45"
Soprano, harp
Commissioned by Helen Webby
Text: Fiona Farrell
Rec: CD Manu 5144

Das Lied von dem Fisch (2015) 7'00"
Soprano, piano
Text: Mary Cresswell
Rec: Rattle Rat-D074
Video: SOUNZ YouTube Channel

Old Mick (2015) 10'00"
Tenor, piano
Commissioned by Christopher Bowen
Text: Denis Glover
Rec: Rattle Rat-D074

Missa Brevis (2019) 7'30"
SATB

Operas

Good Angel, Bad Angel (2005) 60'00"
Mezzo-soprano, baritone, bass, clarinet/bass clarinet, violin, viola, cello
Commissioned by Hebrides Ensemble
Libretto: Ron Butlin, based on the R. L. Stevenson story *Markheim*

The Perfect Woman (2007) 17'00"
Mezzo-soprano, tenor, baritone, picc/ob/cl/bcl/bn/hn/tpt/tbn/perc/2 vlns/vla/vlc/db
Commissioned by Scottish Opera
Libretto: Ron Butlin, freely adapted from Nathaniel Hawthorne's short story *The Birthmark*

Video: SOUNZ website, courtesy of Scottish Opera

The Money Man (2009–10) 60'00"
Mezzo-soprano, mezzo-soprano, tenor, bass, picc(+fl)/ob/ca/cl/bcl/bn/hn/tpt/tbn/perc/2 vlns/vla/vlc/db
Commissioned by Scottish Opera
Libretto: Ron Butlin
Video: SOUNZ website, courtesy of Scottish Opera

Wedlock (2014) 16'00"
Mezzo-soprano, tenor, baritone, picc+fl/ob/cl/bcl/bn/hn/tpt/tbn/perc/2 vlns/vla/vlc/db
Commissioned by Scottish Opera
Libretto: Ron Butlin, inspired by Katherine Mansfield's short story *Millie*

Arrangements

Three Sousa Marches (1979) 8'30"
The High School Cadets, *The Royal Welsh Fusiliers* (No. 3), *The Washington Post*
Picc(+fl)/ob/cl/bcl/bn/hn/tpt/tbn/db

Manhattan Beach by Sousa (1981) 2'00"
Orchestra

Fantasia in F minor K594 by Mozart (2013) 8'00"
Fl/ca/vln/vla/vlc/glass harmonica
Commissioned by the Edinburgh International Festival

Pastoral by Edward Harper (2011)10'00"
Completed from sketches after his death
2220/2200/strings
Commissioned by the Scottish Chamber Orchestra

Graphic scores

Eye Music (1976)
Flute

Nose Music (1977)
Unspecified instrumentation

Feet (1977)
Trombone, hard-soled shoes, tape
Pub: Wait-te-ata Music Press

Organic Music (1979)
3 groups playing any instruments including at least one wood, skin and metal instrument
Rec: Tall Poppies TP039

Ear Music (1980)
To be seen, but not heard
Pub: Wai-te-ata Music Press

Body Music (1994)
A suite of 10 graphic scores
Pub: Wai-te-ata Music Press
Video: SOUNZ YouTube Channel

Soundtracks for film

Taking a line for a walk (1983) 11'00"
A homage to the work of Paul Klee
Animation: Lesley Keen
Video: Lesley Keen YouTube Channel

Orpheus and Eurydice (1984) 6'00"
Animation: Lesley Keen
Video: Lesley Keen YouTube Channel

Invocation (1984) 4'30"
Animation: Lesley Keen
Video: Lesley Keen YouTube Channel

Discography

While some of these CDs may be hard to source, many companies now offer the recordings online or they may be available to borrow from libraries.

British Music Society

Tracey Chadwell's Songbook
BMS420/421CD
Words for Music

Continuum

Paragon Premieres
CCD 1031
Passacagli

Orchestral Music 1
CCD 1033
Concerto for Cello and Orchestra
A Modern Ecstasy

Orchestral Music 2
CCD 1034
O!
Salm
Speak for us, great sea

Delphian Records

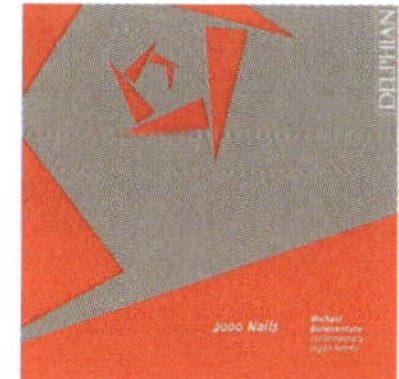

2000 Nails
DCD34013
The Urim and the Thummim

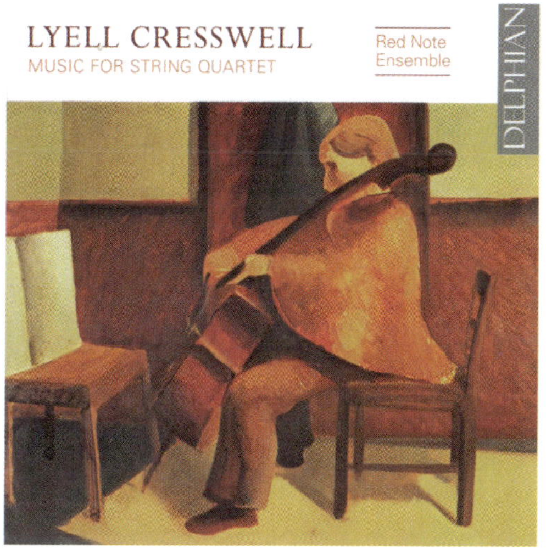

Music for String Quartet
DCD34199
Capricci
Kōtetetete (first movement)
String Quartet

The cover image of my CD Music for String Quartet *is* Cello Player *by Michael Smither. Catherine is the model.*
Delphian Records

First Hand Records

From an Empty Room
FHR139
Lento

Kiwi Pacific Records

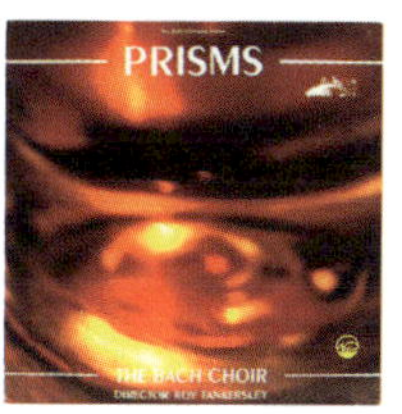

Prisms
SLD-74
O Let the Fire Burn

Linn Records

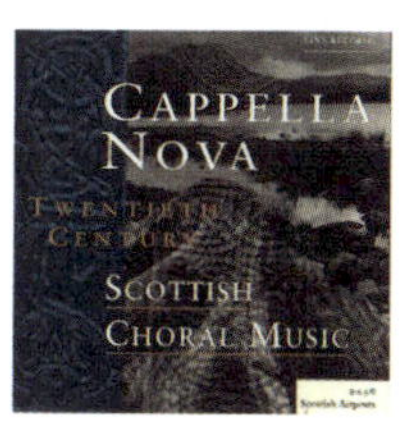

Cappella Nova
CKD 014
To Aspro Pano Sto Aspro

Métier
(part of the Divine Art Recordings Group)

Edward Harper Lyell Cresswell
MSV CD92014
Words for Music
Prayer for the Cure of a Sprained Back
Sextet

Animal Heaven
MSV CD92036
Prayer to Appease the Spirit of the Land

Metronome Recordings

Spectrum 3
Met CD 1053
Apteryx

Morrison Music Trust

Landscapes
MMT2037
Dancing on a Volcano

Naxos

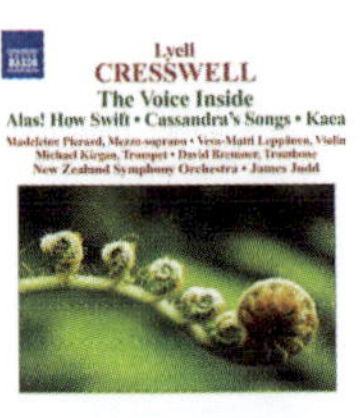

The Voice Inside
8.570824
Alas! How Swift
Cassandra's Songs
Kāea
The Voice Inside
Shadows Without Sun

Landscapes of the Soul
8.573199
Concerto No.1 for Piano and Orchestra
Concerto for Orchestra and String Quartet
I Paesaggi dell'anima

New Zealand Geographic/ SOUNZ

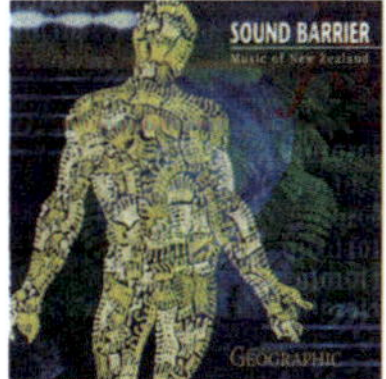

Sound Barrier
The Pumpkin Massacre

NMC Recordings

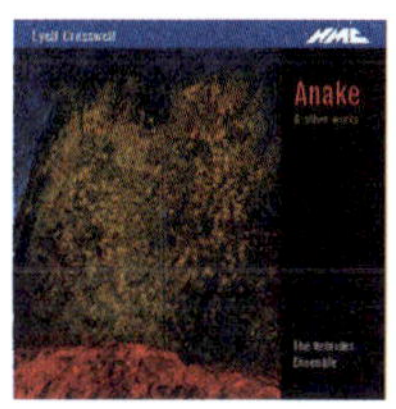

Anake
D077
Acquerello
Anake
Atta
Variations on a Theme by Charles Ives
Whira

The NMC Songbook
D150
A Recipe for Whisky

Ode Records

Under the Southern Cross
Manu 1543/4
Atta

Pluck
Manu 5144
The Harp Sang

Rattle Records

Landscape Preludes
Rat-D046
Chiaroscuro

The Art of Black & White
Rat-D074
Apteryx, The Art of Black and White, Acquerello, Who's Afraid of Red Yellow and Blue, White Relief, Impasto, Mezzotinto, Chiaroscuro, Das Lied von dem Fisch, Four Sentimental Songs, Old Mick, Snatches (from Baptized Generations), Tre Canti

Tall Poppies

Windows in Time
TP039
Organic Music
Soliloquy on a Lambent Tailpiece

Usk Recordings

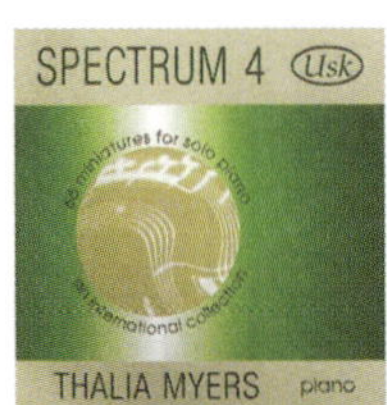

Spectrum 4
Usk 1227CDD
The Leith at Stockbridge

Wai-te-ata Music Press

Chamber Music
WTA002
The Pumpkin Massacre

Chamber Music II
WTA008
Of Whirlwind Underground

Chamber Music III
WTA011
And Every Sparkle Shivering

Notes

Chapter 1

1 'Lumen accipe et imperti', Latin for 'Receive the light and pass it on', is the school motto for Wellington College.
2 Text of 'Hear the Pennies Dropping' is by Fidelia H. DeWitt, published in *Missionary Songs*, Lorenz & Company, 1880.
3 Text from 'Naming of Parts' by Henry Reed was originally published by Jonathan Cape and is reproduced by kind permission of the trustees of the Royal Literary Fund.

Chapter 2

1 *Janet and John* is a series of early reading books for children, widely used in New Zealand schools during the 1950s and 1960s.
2 Published with permission of The Society of Authors.
3 Giselher Klebe (1925–2009) is one of Germany's most distinguished and influential composers, having composed over 140 works including 14 operas and eight symphonies.
4 Margaret Nielsen (1933–2023) was a pianist known for her fine performances of New Zealand music. From 1959 until her retirement in 1993 she taught at the music department of Victoria University (now Te Herenga Waka) where she focused on analysis.
5 In his letter, John North refers to cellist, Wilfred Simenauer who was for many years a member of the New Zealand Symphony Orchestra. The cellist in the recording was in fact Farquhar Wilkinson, a fellow member of the orchestra. He also refers to other composers and performers including New Zealand composer John Rimmer (b.1939), English composer Richard Rodney Bennett (1936–2012), Australian french horn player Barry Tuckwell (1931–2020), American-born conductor Dobbs Franks (1933–2023) who worked extensively in New Zealand and Australia, and New Zealand counter-tenor Geoffrey Coker (b. 1949) who Lyell sang with in the Victoria University Choir and the Bach Choir of Wellington.
6 Darmstadt Ferienkurse is a regular summer event of contemporary classical music in Darmstadt, Germany. It was founded in 1946 and is regarded as a leading international forum for contemporary and experimental music with a focus on composition.
7 John Mansfield Thomson (1926–1999) was a writer, editor and musicologist who specialised in New Zealand music and early music.
8 From *The Swing Era*, Oxford University Press, 1989 (pp263–4).
9 Gustav Ciamaga (1930–2011) was a Canadian composer, music educator and writer best known for his compositions of electronic music.
10 John Weinzweig (1913–2006) was a noted Canadian composer. He is remembered for his advocacy, pedagogy and a compositional style that changed the face of music in Canada.
11 'Esse quam videri' means 'To be, rather than to seem'.
12 Anthony Watson (1933–1973) was a composer and violist. In 1970 he was the inaugural Mozart Fellow at Otago University in Dunedin.

Chapter 3

1 William Frederick Yeames (1835–1918) was a British painter who was born in Russia and studied in Italy before settling in London.
2 Lyell's maternal grandmother, Eleanor Esther Whitehead is not known to be any relation to Gillian Whitehead.

Intermezzo 1

1 Excerpts from *Eye Music, Ear Music, Body Music* and *Feet*, and images from *The Magical Wooden Head* are reproduced with the kind permission of Wai-te-ata Music Press, Te Herenga Waka – Victoria University of Wellington.
2 Karlheinz Stockhausen (1928–2007) was a German composer who is widely acknowledged to be one of the most influential and controversial composers of the last century. He is particularly known for his electronic and serial music.
3 James Fulkerson (b. 1945) is an American trombonist who has had well over 200 works composed for him. He is also a composer.
4 Lysis is a European contemporary music group established in 1970 by composers Roger Dean and John Wallace. It is now part of Australysis, Roger Dean's ensemble based in Australia.
5 Alistair Te Ariki Campbell (1925–2009), born in the Cook Islands, was a poet, playwright and novelist. As well as being one of New Zealand's most distinctive poetic voices, he was a pioneer of Pasifika literature written in English.

Chapter 4

1 Oswald Spengler (1880–1936) is one of the most controversial historians of the twentieth century. His view of history based on the cyclical rise and decline of civilisations gave him the reputation of being an extreme pessimist.
2 Taken by a London physician R. Kenneth Wilson in 1934, the 'surgeon's photograph' of the Loch Ness monster has been responsible for the wide-spread belief that 'Nessie' exists. Ian Wetherell was the first person to expose it as a possible hoax in 1975, although this was not confirmed until 1994.
3 Régime of the Colonels or the Greek junta was a right-wing military dictatorship that ruled Greece from 1967 to 1974.

Chapter 5

1 The International Rostrum of Composers, founded in 1955, is an annual forum of representatives from broadcasting organisations who come together for the purpose of exchanging and broadcasting contemporary music – usually one work from each member country. The representatives select and recommend works which are then broadcast by every member organisation.
2 This example has been transcribed exactly from the score, although the first bar does appear to have a couple of errors. They may be deliberate.
3 The port of Barry near Cardiff was the destination of Geest banana boats from the Caribbean for several decades. Bananas were sprayed with chemicals in the warehouse to speed up the ripening process. There is still a need for trainee banana ripeners.

Chapter 6

1 Marco Boni (b. 1960) is an Italian conductor who began his career as a cellist.
2 Score reproduced with the kind permission of Wai-te-ata Music Press, Te Herenga Waka – Victoria University of Wellington.

Chapter 7

1 Lontano is a London-based contemporary music ensemble founded in 1976 by Odaline de la Martinez and New Zealand flautist Ingrid Culliford. They have performed and recorded many works by New Zealand composers.
2 Sir James MacMillan (b. 1959) is the pre-eminent Scottish composer of his generation and a conductor who performs internationally.
3 Gillian Whitehead (b. 1941) titled a new orchestral work, commissioned by the New Zealand Symphony Orchestra and premiered in October 2022, *Retrieving the fragility of peace*. It is dedicated to Lyell and Catherine.
4 Professor Jack Richards is an active supporter of the arts and music in New Zealand.
5 From *The Necessity for Consolation*, John Cousins, Robert Hoskins, Norman Meehan, Victoria University Press 2019
6 From *The Mysterious Flame of Queen Loana* translated by Geoffrey Brock, published by Vintage.

Editors' note

Before Lyell died in March 2022 he handed over this manuscript to us after we offered to see the book through to publication. If not for the help and support of Lyell and Catherine's friends and family – many of whom are mentioned in Lyell's acknowledgements – this book may have languished in a bottom drawer waiting to be 'excavated'. Our thanks to Te Herenga Waka University Press for offering up their heavy-lifting equipment.

Getting this book into print has been a true collaboration between Lyell's family, friends and the wider composing community.

Thank you to all those who have helped with this publication especially Tim Thornicroft, Iain Matheson and Miriam Meyerhoff. Many others have also helped: Andrew Caldwell, Richard Russell, Lesley Keen, Ron Butlin, Fiona Farrell, Mary Cresswell, John Psathas, Eve de Castro-Robinson, Dominic Saunders, Kate Mead, Roger Wilson, Anthony Young, Michael Norris and Wai-te-ata Music Press, Alan Knowles, Giuliana Carnesecchi, Wendy Campbell, and staff at RNZ Concert and the New Zealand, Scottish and Polish Music Information Centres.

Gillian Whitehead
Scilla Askew